The 2015
Chief Marketing
Officer Handbook

MW00929758

Presented By:

InVert
InVertStrategies.com | 832.800.4295

Marketing Strategies That Work

InVertStrategies.com | 832.800.4295

InVert™
4660 La Jolla Village Dr
Suite 500
San Diego CA 92122

855.350.4295 | 832.800.4295
Concierge@InVertStrategies.com

ISBN-13: 978-1512104486

ISBN-10: 1512104485

To send this book to a friend or colleague visit:

http://InVertStrategies.com/GiftHandbook

Download This Book in Color & Get A Special Bonus!

Claim Your Copy Now

The eHandbook Comes with everything in this book AND you'll get a SPECIAL Invitation to an exclusive online training ONLY Available with your download!

In This Handbook You're Going To Get:

- All of the tools and resources you found in this book in color
- Extra bonus trainings and gifts
- The top producing campaigns, the videos you use, and what types of conversion rates to expect.
- Over $5,000 in Savings and access to new tools as we get them!
- Get key insights on what's working, what's not, and why video marketing is key to growing your business.

~~Only $197~~

Claim Your Complimentary Copy

Go to: InVertStrategies.com/Handbook

* Materials & Labor Fees Extra. See Event Description for Details. Fees based on Location and Date. Average Costs are $137.23.

Table Of Contents:

Pre Selling Is King (7 Steps To Sell An Idea For Profits)

    Discover Your Gift/Expertise

    Explain Your Gift

    Make An Offer

    Get Customers

    Design Your Product or Services

    Deliver To Your Customer

    Repeat With A New Product or Service (or with the same offer later)

The Essentials of Deliverability Both Online & Offline:

    Email Basics:

    Your List Building & Cleansing:

    Opt In's:

    Frequency:

    Here are 11 Alternative marketing avenues other than email:

    Creative attention grabbing ninja tricks & techniques:

Linkedin Marketing

    The Essential Messages

    Target & Connect

    The 3 Touchpoints to Engage Your Connections

    Give A Gift

    Intrigue, Inspire & Convert

    Magnetize Them (Deliver, Make New Offers & Ask for Referrals)

    More on Linkedin Marketing

Types of Campaigns and Their Use

    Lead Capture Campaign

    Consultation Enrollment Campaign

    Insights & Content Delivery Campaign

    Storyboard Campaign

    Commercial Campaign

    Product/Offer Launch

    Ultimate Campaign

"What Types of Video Can I Use In Marketing?"

    Commercial

    Whiteboard

    Opening

    Closing/Ending

    Story

    Opt In/Lead Gen

    Facebook Opt in

    Insights/Content

    Offer/Sales

    Thank You

    Bonus & Upgrade

Event Sponsorship & Speaking Resources
    Lanyard:
    SpeakerMatch:
    Meetup:
    BlogTalk Radio:
    Eventbrite:
My Top Trusted Advisors
    Angelique Rewers - The Corporate Agent:
    Jeff Klubeck - Get A Klu:
    Jon Block & Roni Diaz - Here & Now Network:
    Todd Roth - Cruise One:
    Daniel Rodriguez - Dr. Budget:
    Gail Kraft - Kraft Bravery:
    Carl Logrecco - Innovative Inspirations:

Special Thanks & Dedications:

This book would not have been possible without the help and support of my trusted advisors and the following people:

Barbara Lloyd (Ocean Sanctuaries)

Gyan Penrose Kafka

Caitlin Mueller - My Wife

Paulina Jurzec

Norma Kipp Avendano

Michael Bear

Anne Phelan - Merrett Davies International LLC

CEO Space & Members:
    Rucel Pletado
    Robbin Simons
    Terri Levine
    Hugh Ballou

& More. (Others will be added as we continue to print these, for the most recent dedications download the newest copy of this handbook at InVertStrategies.com/handbook

This book would not have been possible without the help and support of my trusted advisors and the following people:

My mother Barbara Lloyd (Ocean Sanctuaries) I am the person am today because of her. Her guidance and wisdom has been invaluable to me as a person as well as my company. Gyan Penrose Kafka who has kept me aware of actions and their affect on other people and the importance of authenticity in everything that you do. To my business partner Caitlin Mueller who helped me to co-author this book. She has been a huge blessing in my life and a catalyst in taking my business to new heights. Paulina Jurzec for her amazing ability to support us in our mission, vision, purpose and goals achieving them with greater ease and speed. Norma Kipp Avendano who has loved and supported us through our journey and whenever she needs help I know that I am there to support her as well. Thank you Norma for a client relationship that turned into a friendship. There are so many people that I would like to thank for their help on this path to greater success and happiness in both personal and professional life. Each of you reading has made a small yet powerful contribution to the shifts we have seen on a daily to yearly basis. I appreciate you.

3 Gifts for You!

- Free Ticket to Our Thank You Video Workshop
- 100% Off a 50 minute 1-on-1 consultation with our team
- Complimentary Lead Capture Page

Our first Thank You Video Workshop was a lot of fun and we were able to help everyone that attended script, practice, record and post their video on a landing page that was customizable. Hawk is a master when it comes to solving the problems in your unique company and industry. He understands that everyone is different and no two strategies are going to work for the same person. In just 1 hour you are going to get all of his knowledge packed into this session and walk away with massive value. If you are ready to start capturing people that are interested in the services and products you offer then take advantage of our Lead Capture Page.

"BUILD TRUST AND INCREASE RETENTION: LIGHTS, CAMERA, THANK YOU VIDEO WORKSHOP"

You're Invited To Join Us

Join us for this fun filled 2 day event where you will script, record and post a Thank You video.

During The Workshop You're Going To:

- Script and record your Thank You video, to show how much you care about your clients.
- Co-create a solution to show your customers that you're aware of their wants and needs.
- Understand how to interact and ask for referrals by adding value to your viewer.
- Walk away with a product (your edited video integrated in a landing page with links to your website and facebook) on the same day.

~~Tickets are Only $795~~

Claim Your Complimentary Ticket*

Go to: InVertStrategies.com/TyWorkshop-Comp/#Handbook

* Materials & Labor Fees Extra. See Event Description for Details. Fees based on Location and Date. Average Costs are $137.23.

BUSINESS & MARKETING EVALUATION:
"Discover What Your Business Can Do To Increase Your Revenues Now"

Claim Your Complimentary Session Now

Join one of our InVert strategists for a complimentary
1 hour session to discover the solutions for your business.

Our Complimentary Business and Marketing Evaluation:

- We will co-create a marketing and sales strategy.
- Become an Authority and attract more high quality leads and sales for your business!
- Use powerful videos to build your list and sell your products with less effort!

Start Your Application at:
InVertStrategies.com/Analysis/#Handbook

Complimentary Lead Capture Page

Claim Your Complimentary Lead Capture Page Now

It used to be that a website was simply a resource for your leads to learn about your products and services. Now the key is to capture your leads information so that you can directly sell and market to them. This is done through a lead capture page. This page is another type of website which the purpose is to share value in exchange for contact information. The value can be in the form of a video, PDF, webinar, Factsheet, what ever fits your business and expertise.

What you receive:

- **Have a form to attract prospects with your lead magnet (free offer/gift)**
- **Unique website designed to capture lead information**
- **Simple easy to use information for quick editing and setup**

Claim Your Now at:

InVertStrategies.com/LeadCapture/#Handbook

We did a survey of random business owners and managers of mid-sized businesses to better understand what questions and concerns you have. We have 7 topics that were the major challenges related to marketing for most businesses. We also asked business what questions they would ask about marketing. We have answered those questions in this handbook. We did our best to answer all the questions some directly in the insights part, others indirectly throughout the entire handbook.

SINGLE ANSWER

What is the biggest **marketing challenge** you currently have in your **mid sized business?**

Results for all respondents. Weighted data unavailable for this view. (750 responses)
Winner statistically significant.

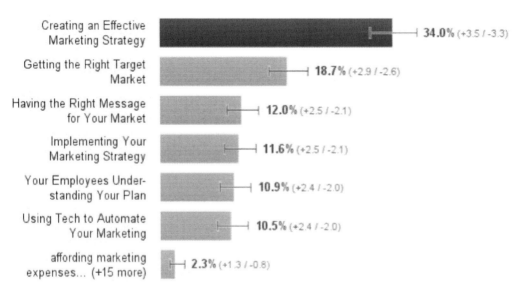

Creating an Effective Marketing Strategy	**34.0%** (+3.5 / -3.3)
Getting the Right Target Market	**18.7%** (+2.9 / -2.6)
Having the Right Message for Your Market	**12.0%** (+2.5 / -2.1)
Implementing Your Marketing Strategy	**11.6%** (+2.5 / -2.1)
Your Employees Understanding Your Plan	**10.9%** (+2.4 / -2.0)
Using Tech to Automate Your Marketing	**10.5%** (+2.4 / -2.0)
affording marketing expenses... (+15 more)	**2.3%** (+1.3 / -0.8)

Methodology: Conducted by Google Consumer Surveys, February 13, 2015 - February 15, 2015 and based on 750 online responses. Sample: People in the "Small/Medium Business Owners and Managers" panel.

Creating an Effective Marketing Strategy
What is one of the most important things a Mid-Sized business needs?

"More than 60% of respondents in our research said they wanted access to advice from people who understand the needs of mid-sized businesses, and/or who have experience of the IT systems that are appropriate for organisations of their size."
~Source for Consulting

Hawk: Strategy, specifically the execution of that strategy, is the #1 factor why a business might lose money, have challenges, become stagnant, or even fail. I've heard "97% of the time a strategy doesn't work its a people problem and only 3% of the time is it the strategy." I believe that is mostly true because the strategy is usually able to get you the results intended. What I disagree on that point is that if you have a strategy that was designed by someone else for a different company, team, or even industry and you expect to get the same results as them you're just kidding yourself.

Think of two twins who grow up in the exact same house, with the same environment, same everything but have two completely different ways of doing the same thing. So what happens when your 300 employees who have different values, come with a different set of skills, and the company culture is different put a system in place that may be for a with 50 employees who don't even use any of the systems that your company has in place.

That is a disaster waiting to happen, and because you have 300 employees it looks like it works just fine. So you might ask yourself are you spending 6 times as much to get the same results as the company with 50 employees? Are your results proportional? Really they should be exponential.

Why is our company culture important to our marketing?

The culture of your company is what defines your brand, your target market, and your messaging.

Hawk: Your marketing comes down to your culture. Your company culture defines everything that you do, and how you do it. A great example of a company who knows their culture and attract their market because of it is an Orange County based health food store called Mothers, and like any of the other name brand health food stores you can get just about anything you want fresh squeezed, right from the vine, or dug out of the ground (I'm not being literal here just an FYI) all sourced from local vendors. I grew up going to this market and at the time I was vegetarian, until I was 16.

I go in one day and I'm craving beef jerky so I go up and ask an employee where I could find some. The look on her face was one of disgust, surprise, and horror that I could come in and ask such a thing. I then realized that everyone of the people in the store were there for great vegetarian or vegan food all willing to spend more than they would if they went across the parking lot to a supermarket with meat.

In essence culture comes down to values, what does your company, your employees and your customers value? Consider that the values of your company attract your employees, and your employees retain your customers.

Why is video marketing so important for engagement and retention?

According to *Wharton School of Business* "Prospects are 72% likelier to buy your products and services when video is used. Video decreases the time it takes a viewer to reach a buying decision by 70%."

Caitlin: Time and time again I find that when I express what business I'm in, people are consistently responding "That's the way of the future." Video marketing is important because video marketing is the future. We are the fortune tellers predicting what will happen next. Video engages your viewers in ways that email campaigns, PDFs, audios, ebooks never will. Video creates TRUST that the person feels they KNOW you before they have even MET you!

Until video became so easy to share, it was nearly impossible to genuinely share what a company actually stood for. You could put it in an article or blog, you could write a long statement, and some people would get it, but around 80% wouldn't. Consider just a few years ago as a company you can spend $100,000's to get a spotlight on TV where you can share who your company is, and what your story is, why you do business, etc. And that was a great way to do it, but it only reached maybe 250,000 viewers of which only 10% are actually in your target market. That is a lot of money for such a low impact.

By hiring the right video marketing company today you can spend the same amount and reach 10 times more people who are genuinely interested and want to buy from you. Think of the possibilities, now when you work with InVert™ and we help you reach the 67% of the market that is untapped and interested in what you have to offer your company will see an increase in revenues.

Hawk: This is extremely important because your clients are going to feel more engaged, more interested, and have a greater sense of trust with your company. We have all heard 'people buy from people who they like, know, and trust.' and your company is a person, a legal person, and it should have a personality, feelings, thoughts, insights, a sense of purpose, and life goals. Just like any other person.

I believe that video is the most effective way to share your company character online. You can connect with people who are hundred or thousands of miles away from you with video. We have seen events filled with people from around the world because of the use of video.

What does video do that no other type of marketing can do? How can I grow our business using video?

According to a recent Aberdeen research study, organizations using video require 37% fewer unique site visits to generate a marketing response.

Hawk: Video has such a big impact in our lives. Imagine you're at a wedding, and there are no videographers, photographers, or even painters to capture the special day. The only thing that would be available to remember it would be the memories of those there. Now the best weddings would be remembered with an incredible story, and it would almost do it justice... Now imagine it was captured on video and that incredible story was too, how would that impact the future story about the wedding to the kids, and grandkids, or even great grandkids.

Video in marketing can do the same thing, it captures the moment, it captures a story, it captures the life and character of your business. Share your story to inspire people to work with you, share your vision to connect with others, give valuable insights to build trust with people.

Video combined with marketing has been proven to increase sales, and decrease the amount of time it takes to engage customer to buy from you.

Reaching the Right Target Market

Should we still use traditional marketing?

The short answer is strategically, Yes. It use to be, "Lets make sure everyone who's in this city get the ad, or anyone who watches this show, or anyone who listens to this radio, reads this magazine, newspaper, etc."

Hawk: Now the number of Gen Y buyers is increasing, which means that you're old ways of marketing are going out the door. I'm in the middle of the Gen Y. We don't care to watch commercials, we are not keen on waiting, and unless it's personal and addressed directly to us we will throw it in the trash. So what does that mean for your traditional marketing. First and foremost know your target market, and I'm not necessarily referring to the customer who comes in and buys. What does that mean?

*A kid (**The Target Market**) is watching a TV show and an ad for this new and amazing cereal comes on 10 times during the 1 hour of TV he gets to watch, and this happens over 3 days until he goes to the store again with his mom (**The Customer**). At the store he sees the display with that same cereal and remembers how much he will like it and asks his mom to buy it for him.*

Back to the key to traditional marketing, if you know that you're market is online, watching web based tv, and only reads books and magazines of interest on a tablet, and listens to online streaming radio, what does that do for you? It does everything, it actually allows you to spend less on your ads and get a greater impact with highly targeted ads.

You see there is a new way to do traditional marketing, it's more targeted, less expensive PER lead, and you have more tools at your fingertips to get to their fingertips.

The key was always and will always be to go from offline to in store, the key is that in store may be online now.

This is really an entire book in itself. I will be going more in depth on Direct Marketing in the next section. If you would like to discuss this further you can schedule a strategy session with our team. Call 832.800.4295 to set that up. Mention this book and get a $500 discount.

Where has direct mail seen the greatest improvements and how I best to leverage them?

Direct mail is one of the most forgotten pieces of marketing that you can use and when done wrong can be overly expensive.

Hawk: I'm going to go over 3 tactics based on 3 groups of target markets. These all assume that you have acquired (either by permission or by purchasing or by researching) their information in full.

The Manager/Executive/Owner (B2B): This one is simple and easy and can get very expensive.

1. Get Their Attention
   a. Send a value adding resource If you can hand write it, or if you have bad handwriting like me handwrite part of it as neatly as possible.
   b. Label it Sensitive Information for their eyes only.
   c. Send it overnight FedEx
   d. (if you have their permission to send them an email) Email them to let them know you have sent them a sensitive package for their eyes only it will arrive tomorrow.

CTA (Call to Action): "No need to respond, you're very busy, please just enjoy this resource. For the resource I Recommend A, B and C. I will follow up with you in X Days (Based on your industry and resource)." Leave your contact info below your signature to give them the opportunity to get back to you if needed.

2. Follow the steps below for B2P, except you're going to do it in another FedEx Overnight labeled sensitive.

Business to Professional ($100k+ Annually): This is where it starts to get less expensive and a little more tricky. The letter needs to be address to them, and written on the front of the envelope. This must <u>SCREAM</u> Personal, and you will get their attention and fast. Also a handwritten note from someone at your office or ordered from a hand writing service that gives them an uplift in their day.

CTA: "Lets talk, what does your calendar look like next week at Time X or Time Y. Attached is a postage paid postcard with an ID Number to keep your information secured. You can add any additional info to it prior to sending it. Please check the appropriate time and have it mailed today. Thank you for your time." Leave your number and contact info so they can call you right then and there if they want too.

Business To Consumer: This is the hardest to get to because they're the most marketed to, but the cheapest by far. I still recommend acquiring a targeted list and send them an address letter. This can all be printed. Make sure you use appropriate merge fields. Ask them to call or visit online.

Why is YouTube so Powerful? What's the difference between YouTube & Vimeo? Should I use both?

According to YouTube itself "More than 1 billion unique users visit YouTube each month. Over 6 billion hours of video are watched each month on YouTube—that's almost an hour for every person on Earth."

According to Build Wealth as of July 2014 "Only 0.2% of all websites in the world use Vimeo."

Caitlin: I would absolutely recommend using both Vimeo and YouTube because each has a different audience. YouTube has incredible viewership and now that Google owns YouTube the search function is even greater. The way to integrate Vimeo is reach the people who are not on YouTube and increase your SEO at the same time. It is also primarily used in the professional world to host videos.

Hawk: Youtube has a huge viewership so the impact it can have on your business is simply incredible. YouTube has some of the most amazing marketing tools integrated into it and its installed on most phones too. They also recently designed an app that helps businesses track their views right from their phone.

I believe that if you have videos you MUST be on YouTube, if you're not you're missing out on a HUGE market. I can almost guarantee that your target market is on YouTube, unless you're targeting cave people. Do a few simple things to make your channel better:

1. Have great insights and content to share with your community.
2. Work with other YouTube channels to co-promote each other.
3. Always have a Call To Action on every video.
4. Post on a regular basis, the more consistent the better.

YouTube and Vimeo are both important. Vimeo is really an untapped market, that you can use to broaden your marketing without spending a bunch of extra money. Vimeo is more of a professional video network, that has some great subscription features that allow you to charge for people to buy your video(s). If you decide to use Vimeo you need a Pro account, otherwise you're not able to leverage it, your videos won't be mobile optimized, etc. So just pay the $200 per year for your account.

When do I share my videos on Facebook, Twitter, and Linkedin?

InVert's research over the months of June and July 2014 has shown that an average of 13 out of 15 posts in the facebook news feed are videos or a link to an article, usually with a video. That number seems to be increasing, and rapidly. We expect that by the end of 2014 that 19 out of 20 posts seen in the news feed will be videos or links to articles with videos. The key to sharing your videos on Facebook, Twitter, Linkedin is sharing them when they are done, at the beginning of each campaign and most importantly using both your introductory commercial and opt in videos as ads to attract people to visit your website, blog or anywhere you can post an opt in box.

Caitlin: Share your posts right as they happen. Something that is a day old is old news in Social Media. I would recommend getting videos up within a week after an event and post periodically as the event is happening. The same goes for photos.The number of postings on Facebook should be about once a day, Twitter up to five times a day and LinkedIn once a week.

Hawk: The number of video posts on Facebook is staggering, and is only going to get more impressive. Your business will thrive off of videos, and were not talking about a video that costs you $10,000 for every 60 seconds to make. It still has to be professionally created, but in the right way. It is important to have a well designed commercial that's placed right, a raw video can have a much bigger impact when it shows you authentically, the character of your company, the story of why your business is here to support others, what you can teach them, and how you can solve their problem.

The bad thing is that anyone can pick up a camera and shoot a video, anyone can upload a video to youtube. According to YouTube "100 hours of video are uploaded to YouTube every minute." which is a testament that your video will get lost in the stream if you're not using your videos right. Imagine that for <u>every 60 seconds</u> of video you want to use for your business there is about <u>5 to 10 hours</u> of professional production time (so upwards of 20 hours for DIY), not to mention that you need to have a long list of equipment that ends up costing upwards of $3,000.

I believe that all successful people hire and delegate tasks they're not experts in accomplishing. The good thing is that a video marketing campaign isn't expensive to get it done right. You can get professional 'Natural' videos that start anywhere between $1000 to $2000 per 60 seconds of final video, which includes everything done for you, a squeeze page, website integration, etc. And it only takes you about 20 to 30 minutes of your time to get it done. And on the higher end you can get professional 'Commercial' videos that start anywhere between $7,000 to $10,000 per 60 seconds of final video, including everything done for you, fully edited, with royalty free music, hosting, etc. this will take you about 2 or 3 hours of your time.

Having the Right Message for Your Market

What is the benefit of starting a pre-launch for something we have never offered?

"Apple Announces Record Pre-orders for iPhone 6 & iPhone 6 Plus Top Four Million in First 24 Hours" ~Apple's Website

Hawk: Preselling is the ONLY way I will launch a new product. As a matter of fact I got paid to write this book. People pre-purchased the book so I could write it for them. What a great concept.

Do you want to spend $10,000 developing a new product, service, or program that you have no customers for OR do you want to ask all of your customers to buy in advance (for a discount of course) and have your customers put up the $10,000. The other component is your market will tell you exactly what they want know, hear, and get from the purchase so you can really hone in on your messaging.

The question I get most often about this is "What if we don't deliver or scrap the project completely?"
First you say "Sorry" and then you do the following 3 things (in order, until the offer is accepted)
1) Let them know of the changes and give them the option to choose between waiting or becoming a Beta Tester (if you scrap the project offer them something else that you have that solves a problem they have.)
2) Offer a store credit at the FULL retail value.
3) Offer them the Full refund + a store credit for about 20% of the original payment.

We have an entire section on this later in the handbook.

How can I get people to engage with our videos? What drive people to buy online?

According to Forbes Insight "59% of senior executives would rather watch a video than read text. Of those 59%, about 65% of those who view a video click through to visit the vendor website, 45% report that they contacted a vendor after seeing an online video ad, and about 50% went on to make a purchase for their business."

Lets do the math on that. 59 out of 100 people in your target market want to watch your video, 65% of those 59 people, about 38 people, will click to see what you are offering. About 27 will call to ask you questions before they make a decision to buy, and 29 of the original 59 will buy from you during that session.

Caitlin: People decide whether or not they will watch a video within 3 seconds. That means in 3 seconds you must GRAB their attention to continue watching. Once over that hurdle, you content must continue to be above and beyond because while they are watching your video they are checking email, on Facebook, have at least five different tabs open...you get the idea. Your online viewership is your most DISTRACTED audience! Once you engage give people what they want. It's really very easy, simply ask and they will tell you.

Hawk: You get people to engage with your videos by making sure they're interested in what you have to offer. That means selecting the right target market for your campaign; if you need to, do some market research. The fact is that every marketing campaign is only as successful as the relationship between the desires of the target market you are advertising to and the product or service you're trying to sell them.

If your campaign isn't producing you results then you have two options.
1) You change your target market to match your campaign.
2) You change your campaign to match your target market.

They will both produce results for you, if you have the budget I would do both. Start with the first one and then move of to the second on. You already have a campaign designed for another market and you just need the right market to make it produce and make you money, the second is to attract your ideal client you need to make some shifts in your campaign and you will produce much more profitable results over the long term.

I would have to say that if 59% of executives would rather watch a video, consumers are even more interested in watching a video, or are at least more likely to take action. 29 out of every 59 people who watch your video are great odds. Consider this, you are selling a $37 product. You spend $10 per person who clicks spending a total of $590 and you sell 29 people a $37 product generating a total revenue of $1,073. Your profits are $483, how many people can you send this to? Trick question, send it to an unlimited number of people in your target market. Lets just say that you spent $10 for 100 people to see it, you still profited $73 and you now have 29 new clients you can offer additional products and services to. To sum it up you can make more money with marketing a video than you can by putting your money in your bank.

How do I set our company apart from our competitors in the eyes of our clients?

According to Ivan Misner in Fox Business article on networking "Possibly the most important piece for success in networking. Tell stories." He goes on to share about an encounter Robert Dickman, author of *The Elements of Persuasion*. "He taught me the formula for a good story: 1) A story is a fact, 2) wrapped in an emotion. 3) that compels us to take action, and 4) that transforms us in some way."

Your clients will remember your story because of the emotions that move them to work with you instead of your competitors. Anyone can do transactional selling, its simple, buy the lowest price products and sell as many of them as possible with the lowest profit margin to beat out your competition in a price war. Or you can shift your message and still offer lower prices but not the lowest price. A customer will pay more when they know the service provided is in alignment with the increase in prices.

Caitlin: First and foremost don't compete. Collaborate. Set yourselves up as the experts, you know the industry backwards and forwards. Give! Give! Give! Show them your value and they will buy. I'll give an example:

I had been going to many seminars and there were coaches offering their services. But they didn't really give me any value as to why I should work with them. That is until Angelique Rewers. As soon as she stepped on stage within five minutes she gave VALUE! And I got resourceful to buy her product. Once I did that she continued to give insights that added to my success. By the time I got to her event (which was included with the program) she had given so much value that I purchased again. All of that set her apart from other business coaches in the industry. That's what you need to do.

Hawk: I believe your story to be one of the most compelling and moving components of any business. I handed a company a $15,500 cashiers check because I liked a story and I saw value in what they were offering. The great part about a story is that it will attract your target market, it will define your company, it will set you out, it will make you different. Read my story on the next page, it's broken down into the key elements of a story.

Caitlin and I were at an illusions show seeing all sorts of magic tricks and illusions. During nearly the entire show I was unimpressed and somewhat bored, but there were 3 parts of the show I remember. All 3 had an emotional story that gave a background to his act, one nearly made me cry. He shared a story of his grandfather who had passed away and expressed his gratitude and appreciation for him. If it weren't for those components of the show I would have thought it was a complete waste of time.

Hawk Mikado's Story

- Past - Struggle:
  - Call: Growing up I traveled the world, visiting 13 countries and nearly 1/2 of the US. I saw people all around the world who felt misunderstood, and have a message to share with the world.
  - Pit: By the time I was *18, I had built 6 companies* and ran 3 family businesses, trying to find my way, my voice, my purpose in life. I had everything, I knew everything... Or at least I thought so for a while. I found my passion and purpose in growing businesses, but I began to feel misunderstood myself. To escape from ridicule of my peers, and some of my teachers I began drinking, and doing drugs. Eventually I lost sight of my passion and purpose. I lost all of my so called friends, my girlfriend at the time. I spiraled down, I wanted to die because I felt more misunderstood than ever. I drank OJ and Vodka for days and I didn't eat anything else; on Christmas I was admitted into the hospital.... That night *my heart stopped 3 times, I died 3 times, and luckily I was revived 3 times.*

- Present - Realization:
  - Turning Point: When I woke up the doctor walked in and said to me "You need to change your life, or you will die"... I made a decision to commit my life to supporting people to live their passions. I started to work on my 1 on 1 practice. I found I needed *leaders to share their wisdom* to support me in growing and being able to **communicate in a way that everyone understood me.** Since then I have been mentored by *leading experts* and received the training I needed to be able to support companies to share their message in a compelling, inspiring, and value driven way and create an environment that is conducive of great success.

- Future - Where are you going:
  - Breakthrough: I live *my life with a purpose* of enjoying everything I do. My true passion is growing businesses with unique strategies and systems that consistently get results. I personally have had many failures, challenges and learnings that I'm able to bring to the table and support companies grow. Over the last 3 years, I have had greater and greater success. I was able to bring in $45,000 in revenue within 1 hour after a 2 day event for Success Academy, a speaking company, as a consultant. I helped another consulting company, Here & Now Network, build and launch a campaign that resulted in a 93% conversion on the front and 30% on the back, generating an additional $5,400 in revenue. That company has seen over a 500% ROI from working with us.

- Call to action:
  - Give me a call at 832.800.4295 when you're interested in having your business see a great ROI from having the right strategy to Engage, Convert, and Inspire your market.

Implementing Your Marketing Strategy

Mobile! Mobile! Mobile! and what we need to know on that front:

Speaking of Text Message Marketing there is a lot more that goes into mobile marketing then just texts. In our email marketing campaigns alone we see over 70% of our opens are done from a mobile phone, over 10% from a tablet, and the other 20% vary to all different platforms.

There are 3 major parts about your marketing that you need to make sure are mobile or you will lose up to 80% of your market within 3 seconds.

1. All of your Emails, Websites, Logos, Etc. MUST MUST MUST Be Mobile "Responsive" which basically means their size adjusts based on the size of the screen they're being displayed on.

2. When placing ads online you can always check to see what it will look like on a mobile device, tablet and a computer. The mobile part is crucial, you generally have about 120 characters before it cuts you off and adds the **...** and the rest of your message is cut off. Your call to action needs to be in that very first sentence, and done in a way that is compelling and adds value to the clicker.

3. Test everything on the following 5 platforms before you send anything out: (Each platform has multiple formats that you should test on but you must test on at least one, the one the majority of your target market uses)
   a. Mobile Phones: Both Android & iPhone
   b. Tablets: Android Tablet, iPad, & Windows Tablet
   c. Mac: Safari Browser & Mail
   d. PC: Internet Explorer and Outlook
   e. Google: Chrome & Gmail

Multi-media marketing integration:

Define Multi-Media: Any media that is accessible on multiple platforms; including Social Media, Blogs, SEO, Pay Per Click, Landing Pages, Webinars, Podcasts, and the MOST Common is **Video**.

Hawk: HOLY (Insert your expression of overwhelm here), there really is a lot of stuff to consider when working with multi media, especially when it comes to marketing it, and even more so with integrating everything together. So what can you do about it and how can you make it all integrate into your systems easily.

*The very first project to integrate is map out on a whiteboard (so you can easily erase) your process from acquisition to each conversion. Lets look at **Video** since that's what most of you thought of when thinking of Multi-Media marketing.*

3 Major components to integrate all Multi-media into your marketing. 1) your platform, 2) your host, 3) your system.

The platform is where your multi-media lives, for instance when you post on Facebook the platform is Facebook the multi-media is your post. In terms of video it comes down to 3 major players, YouTube (Most Common), Vimeo (More Professional), and Amazon a3 (More customizable).

The host is normally your website, or landing page. It's where people go to see the multi-media. The host can also be a platform.

The System is where all of the information is kept about the multi-media in both the host and the platform. This can also be part of the host and the platform as well.

What kinds of video equipment should I use? How do I record a video and market our videos?

Your top 5 things you need are a camera, lights, microphone, editing software, and most importantly a script to follow.

Caitlin: Equipment is irrelevant if you don't know how to use it. A professional with an iPhone and an amateur with a $10,000 camera, well you will see a difference. Know the basics of video, and with whatever you have apply them. A good story is the key to video. Make sure the audio is good because that will make or break the success of the video as well. As far as marketing a video goes: PROMOTE! PROMOTE! PROMOTE! Before the video is shot, once the video is posted and consistent promotion after that.

Hawk: First I want to say that unless you're a professional Videographer or want to be, leave it to the Pro's. Now I'm usually in front of the camera, I love being on camera so I have a different experience than the camera person. I know that there are some very key components to recording a video before you market it.

Start with a well crafted script, to ONE person, to your perfect customer. Personally I hate scripts, I think they're annoying, and inauthentic. But all of my best and most authentic videos are ones I scripted and recorded knowing exactly what I was going to say. I write it word for word, read it out loud 5 or 10 times, record myself 2 or 3 times on audio. Then select bullet points out of each main point, and just go with the flow when I get on camera.

The second most important part of every video is an AMAZING Microphone. The fact is that if you don't have good audio you don't have a video. We've had to throw out countless videos or have someone spend countless hours editing because there was something wrong with the audio. Make sure that you test your audio and listen to a playback of the video while you're 'on location' where you're recording your video. The Camera, Lights, and Editing software is up to you, but make sure it's high quality. You need to end up with a professional video to market it to your customers.

Marketing your videos is a whole other beast, and unless you're a marketer hire a company to do it for you. We understand what you need to do to get your videos seen bringing in the revenues. The biggest money saver is to only spend money marketing your introductory commercials and opt in videos that will lead your target market into other videos, and inspire them to buy at the right time.

Your Employees Understanding Your Strategy

How can my employees effectively implement the strategies we put in place?

Earlier this statistic was shared: "97% of the time a strategy doesn't work its a people problem and only 3% of the time is it the strategy."

Hawk: I thought it was interesting that only 11% of companies think that this is their biggest marketing challenge, when it is often the largest problem of them all. Before I address the technical aspects of the deliverability best practices, lets look at leadership. Your Leadership is the backbone of your company and your team. When I attended a leadership course, each week we had a new speaker who shared their experiences in leadership positions and how they got there. I remember one gentleman who built a construction company of over 2000 employees before he sold it, and he knew every single one, he worked in the field with them, he got dirty with them, and he bought everyone of them lunch.

His experiences came from over 10 years of bad employers and knowing exactly what he never wanted to happen in his company. He chose to lead by example, he made sure that the people on the front line where respected as the most important people in his company. His company structure was an upside down pyramid. He felt that his workers were the top (where the CEO usually is) and he (the CEO) was at the bottom. And while an upside down pyramid wouldn't seem very stable, it was his workers that stabilized and strengthened the company. They were the ones who made the final decisions in the field and they deserved the most credit for the good work.

He had systems in place, very good ones, that made his company a great profit. The systems were so good they had people from competitors companies begging to come work for his company, and they would work for less money too. He understood that his systems were no better than the systems of his competitors, BUT the way his crews implemented and executed those systems was the defining feature that set his company apart from the rest, the one that made it extraordinary. Those systems were people systems, the system of how he treated his people.
There were 3 major components to his success with his people understanding the work:

1. *He openly praised good work and showed it as an example.*
2. *He took responsibility for bad work and privately <u>discussed</u> the challenge and how to improve in the future, never placing blame on the other person, he always asked them what they felt went wrong, and how they could have prevented it or fixed it.*
3. *He did the same work as his employees and expected that every leader in his company followed the same principles.*

Using Tech to Automate Your Marketing

Does it matter what technology and CRM our company is using and why?

There are 2 things that your technology should do for you:

1. Make your life easier, it should take your team less time than if you were to do it by hand, and cost less than if you were to hire someone else (a consultant) to do it with a pen, paper, and some staples.

2. Your technology should be intuitive and the person using it should be able to understand how it works. Not to mention be able to easily use it.

Hawk: Our tech is awesome, we use one system as the backbone of everything we do at our company called InfusionSoft (GetMMC.com/InfusionSoft) and it integrates with everything else we have. As a matter of fact, if it doesn't integrate we won't buy it. InfusionSoft has saved me personally over 20 hours PER WEEK in work. It is also our email marketing system, CRM, and eCommerce platform. It and the other tools (found in the resource section) help me do bookkeeping, appointment setting, social media marketing, and so much more.

If your technology isn't giving you a leg up then you might not have the right tech. One major concern for companies who have an older system that requires a lot of manual input is the time and money it takes to move over. Yes you have to train employees, update websites, etc. which may take an average of 4 hours per employee. You can continue to have employees who are losing an hour per week of productivity because they are manually transferring documents, or a sales team who loses a client because they didn't get an automated notice to tell them who they need to follow up with today.

The cost to go to a new system like Infusionsoft, especially with us as your implementor, is much less expensive than any system you have in place now.

What is the best way to get right to our customer and bypass the barriers?

"SMS is fast and very effective. 97% of all text messages are opened and read. SMS is not a replacement for email, but a powerful addition to it, especially when your messages are time sensitive. Using a text-in call to action gives your prospects an easy way to respond. You want them to take action the moment they're inspired - precisely when they see your offer. Text messaging is the perfect solution when they only have access to a mobile device. "
-Social Fuse SMS PlayBook (GetMMC.com/SmsPlayBook)

Hawk: When we started to get in front of our prospective clients by speaking and capturing their info with a text message we saw an increase in engagement and results. The quick answer is find places to speak, get interviewed, etc, and when you do make an offer for a gift via text message. Go ahead and try it, Text Video to 96000.

From there you want to follow up with ALL of the following:

1) Call their phone
2) Email Them
3) Text Them
4) Find them on Linkedin/Facebook and friend them so you can talk with them their.

If you want a more in depth conversation around this Text Video to 96000 and schedule a time to speak.

What tools are best converting right now for list growth?

InVert™ uses 4 of the most amazing tools in the marketplace, one is the backbone, one is our online, and one is our offline tool, and one is for speaking to groups or can be used in radio/tv ads.

First and formost you MUST Get Infusionsoft (GetMMC.com/InfusionSoft). It is the master of automation. It makes everything from lead generation, to email marketing, to eCommerce, to paying out commissions as simple as possible. WARNING: I put in campaign maps later on in the book, set up of these is crucial to have them right or you'll spend a long time trying to figure out what went wrong. Hire a team of InfusionSoft experts like us to help you setup your system, AND train your team to use the system properly.

Second is our online Lead generation tool. LeadPages (GetMMC.com/LeadPages) You can easily set up your landing pages, heck we use it for all of our main websites too (InVertStrategies.com) When you use us to set up your Infusionsoft we also set up your opt ins inside of LeadPages. There are multiple options for this.

Third is our offline lead generation tool, its really a tool that we use when generating a lead offline during networking or other types of meetings, and it also integrates into (you guessed it) InfusionSoft. It's called MeetMe (GetMMC.com/MeetMe) and it's our scheduling program. It's connected directly to the calendar of each of our team members so they can book appointments with the appropriate people. We have a very particular practice that is important for every business to put in place when networking or meeting with someone, here it is: Set An Appointment By The END of Your Conversation. To set up an appointment with me right now go to meetme.so/HawkMikado

Fourth and final crucial lead generation tool we use is SocialFuse. (GetMMC.com/SmsPlayBook) Which is a text messaging platform that also integrates into InfusionSoft. It really is the most effective tool you can use in marketing today when you're speaking with a large crowd, playing a radio ad, a TV ad, and it can even be used in Print Ads (when done correctly.) Text InVert to 96000.

Finding the Budget for Marketing & Measuring the ROI.

How do I get the best return on my campaign? how long does it take to get roi?

Marketing is a series of successes and failures that you have to adjust to get the perfect campaign.

Hawk: The very first thing you need to do is evaluate your business, your culture, your systems, and budget to figure out what you have at your fingertips. Once you know what you have then you can map out your plan of action. You start implementing right away, and you test it for at least 45 days. About every 7 days or so you want to check in on your campaign and see what's going great and what's not. If you find a part that's not working so well then you will only make a minor change like messaging or workflow.

E.g. You drive 100 leads to your campaign. 30% of Customers buy offer #1 and 20% upgrade to offer #2. You email them to let them know about offer #3 and find that only 5% buy, and you're expecting 10%. You adjust your messaging and send out to get another 7% (12% total). You then offer an upgrade to offer #4 and only 2% buy, you find out that there's a challenge with the process to buy offer #4, you fix it and you email out again to get another 3% keeping you on target. You can expect to see the majority of your ROI from your campaign within 7 days from sending an email or making a call. Now when I refer to your ROI in this case I'm referring to an action being taken. It could be a purchase or an appointment set or webinar watched.

When it comes to Financial ROI that really depends on your sales cycle. For instance we have a 3 month sales cycle from lead to appointment to purchase. Here are some ROI from lead times that I've personally seen based on price. There are a lot of other factors that can either accelerate or slow this time down:

(The % next to the box is an average conversion rate the timeline is how long we see it can take)

	Cold Leads 2%	Warm Leads 5%	Hot Leads/Recent connections 10%	Referrals/speaking 20%
<$500	45 Days	30 Days	15 days	3 to 7 days
<$2,000	90 Days	60 Days	45 Days	14 days
<$10,000	240 Days	180 Days	150 Days	60 days

How can I pay less for advertising and get more bang for your buck?

The quick answer is that your advertising will always cost you proportionally to the potential return for your investment. There is a bit more to it though. First, you can always buy remnant space, or lower cost ads, however you want to ask yourself what return with that lower costing ad? The first question you should really be asking yourself before you buy an ad is: What is your goal for the ad, AND what is the expected return for that ad?

There are 3 sides to this:

1. *The ad you pay less for gets placed in the prime time and you get the best Return. BUT you have no control over this.*

2. *Your ad runs at the worst possible time and you don't get a worthwhile return, or potentially any.*

3. *My favorite is using your ad budget for more targeted ads.*

   Lets look at this further:
   > *You buy two ads for $10,000 each. The first gets you in front of 100,000 people (1,000 of your target*
   market, and only 100 are interested in what you're offering)

   > *The second gets you in front of 2,000 people all in your target market and about 500 are interested in what*
   you're offering and want to buy.

   > *In this case, because the goal is more leads the second option was the best fit. If you were looking for*
   general visibility (not targeted visibility) then the first option would have been your best fit.

What are creative ways to fund my marketing when I have a budget under $10,000?

There are 3 major ways to fund your business marketing initiatives. #1 is Pre-sell, #2 is a Launch Campaign, #3 is joint venture events.

#1: Pre-sell is the most popular and the least costly. We go more in depth on how to do this later, the basics rely on 3 components the first is identifying the needs of your clients and prospects. This is key because you want to get your offer out to the most people without having a lot of information about what you're offer is. This is designed to help you get market feedback. A great example of that would be the iWatch. Once people purchase let them know the estimated delivery date, offer them beta access if appropriate and then ask them for feedback. "If there was one feature that you'd like to see in this what would it be?"

#2: A launch campaign is great for an offer that you have already developed. Use it to add value and build your list to get traction, you will then make an offer for a discount in a specific time period. This launch campaign can be run every 3 or 4 months to re-engage past clients.

#3: Joint venture events are a great way to get local prospects to join you and for your joint venture partners to attract their customers. You have the power of a referral and the credibility of being the expert (speaker) all in one key component. This is also one of the most expensive ways BUT you only pay once you get the new customer.

The most powerful campaign is a launch campaign driving everyone to a joint venture event where you pre-sell.

How do I attract and convert higher paying clients?

Online and offline are both the same concept just in different places. Online we use and recommend Linkedin because over 49% of LinkedIn Users Have Household Income Over $100K per year and are decision makers. I use this stat because it has never dropped below this in the last 5 years and is expected to rise even from where it is today.

On linkedin you can connect directly with high level decision makers. This is key to attracting them because you want to be able to show them you're an expert in what you do and it's easier to do so when you're not getting caught on the gatekeeper all the time.

When it comes to offline we recommend hosting an executive invitation only event where you can host your specific target market and discuss a problem that they're currently having. Events are more relevant because you know that the topic is something that they're considering in the next 3 months.

The easiest way to fill your event is invite your prospects from Linkedin to join you at your event.

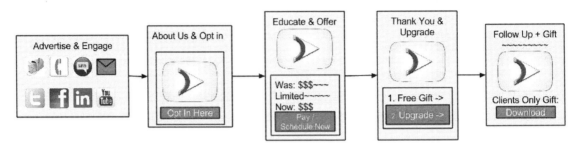

The Basics to Marketing & Sales Funnel Automation

1. **Advertise & Engage**
   - Posts Ads online and offline.
   - Have Your JVs send emails
   - Email your current list
   - Message your connections on Social Media
2. **"About Us" & Opt in**
   - Share your story
   - What are they going to get when they opt in
3. **Educate & Offer**
   - What's the problem
   - How do you solve the problem
   - Offer to solve their problem for them
4. **"Thank You" & Upgrade**
   - Simply saying "Thank You" for buying goes a long way
   - Ask them to upgrade their recent purchase
5. **Follow Up + Gift**
   - Connect with them on a regular basis
   - Offer them a gift that brings them through this process again

Your campaign is the life of your strategy, the workflow, the heartbeat. If your campaign doesn't have all of these components then you're missing a huge part of your market. The easiest way to do this is through videos, though it isn't necessary. There are plenty of materials that aren't done with video that get people to take action. (Like this one.) I will refer to the "Viewer" they could be reading, listening or watching the content. Each of these 7 components are only as important as the message they deliver to the "Viewer" and you will see us play around with these things from time to time. By combining two parts together, or switching them around, or making a barrier you see who is truly serious about the offer. For instance requiring a credit card on a free item, or having a 7 page application to get a consultation with us. Those are just a few. Now we're going to dive into the reason around each one of these, and give you some templates for how to do it. My disclaimer to our templates: They are really guidelines that give you something to follow, use the templates a few times, then you will understand how to get creative and innovative with your ideas.

1. Your Story

Why is your story AND your company story so important? Think about it. Really stop and think about the last time you heard a story, maybe it was one of your grandparents or a friend, or possibly a complete stranger. How did the story make you feel? What was the very next thing you wanted to do?

These questions are all questions the you can ask yourself when you're crafting your story. I demonstrated a story on the page before this so you can see what the "Hero's Journey" looks like. NOTE: The Pit of your story doesn't' have to be a life and death situation, it just has to convey a challenge that you didn't think you were going to overcome.

Now it's Time to Create your own story (Or your Company's Story):
- (optional) What are things like now:
- Told in the Past tense- Struggle:
  - The Call - What is the reason why you started this journey
  - Pit - The challenge you didn't think you could overcome
- Told in the Present - Realization that you could overcome the challenge
  - Turning Point - When you were able to overcome that challenge
- Told in the Future - Where are you going
  - Breakthrough - Why things are great and are going to get better
- Call to action - What do you want the "Viewer" to do next

2. Your Opt In Gift Offer

If you want to get people in your virtual door so they come into your physical doors the "Gift" is the fastest way to do this. **It MUST Be a HUGE Value Add!** This book for instance (which is available on amazon for $197), we are literally sharing our best stuff. We know that if you love this, we also know that you can hire our company to come in, make you a lot more money and a larger ROI with a customized strategy. With our team implementing those strategies along side your team we know that you will get even better results.

Before we get to the "How to Script it" section lets make 3 things very clear:
1. You need to know what your target wants? Why do they want it? When will they use it? How long will it take them to get through it? When will they take action?
2. When you ask for an opt in, get their first name, email AND Phone (leave the phone field as optional though). If someone won't give you their first name, they aren't really interested (most of the time.) If you go to any of ours you'll notice we ask for First, Last Name, "Business Email" and "Business Cell Phone" to get more qualified leads.
3. If someone is already on your email list, then DON'T make them opt in again when you send them an email letting them know about a new free gift, just give it to them. You can ask for additional information if you want to though, for instance phone, address, favorite animal, etc.

Do you want to (Express benefit 1)

"My Name is (Name), (Identity), and (Title) of (Company/Brand)"

Big Fat Claim: Provide (TARGET) with (Product) so (Benefit)

How long have you wanted (What your offer solves for them)

(The Struggle/Experience to why this was made)

Benefits: (My Solution - the offer)

Proof: My Results [up to 3 case studies, testimonials, mention of results]

Offer: (Solution Framework - how will this solve their problem)

Scarcity: Do's & Don't - (Why do they want it, {and why don't they want it} [disqualifier to get higher quality opt in's])

Call to action: (A clear and concise single call to action. What are they going to do next?)

3. The Insights (Content)

Your expertise, your insights, your projections of the future are THE BEST content in the world. This book is a great example of this. Consider the Q & A Section above, we took someone elses content and added our insights to it.

There are 2 major benefits of using insights as content.
1) Your company is known as an expert because it has an opinion about how things work.
2) It takes a lot less time to think up new things, so that means you can innovate the tools that are already around you and make them better.

NOTE: There is a time and a place for innovating and creating "new things" and you should do it about 4 times per year, the rest of the year is spent giving insights.

Idea: Poise the question, comment, "Fact" or key point. Then commend them on at least one thing related to their key point.

New Idea: Give why you believe what you believe.

Old Problem: Share the problem and some of its underlying symptoms to the initial point.

New Solution: Share the innovations you've made on the initial idea.

Benefit: Lay out how it will benefit others to believe this too.

Proof: 3-5 case studies, testimonials, mention of results. Each should solve symptom of the problem, not the problem itself.

Offer: (Solution Framework - how will this solve their problem)

Scarcity: Do's & Don't - (Why do they want it, {and why don't they want it} [disqualifier to get higher quality opt in's])

Call to action: (A clear and concise single call to action.) What are they going to do next?

4. Your Offer / Call To Action

Your offer is self explanatory, but just in case...its what you're selling. "Selling" is not necessarily an exchange of MONEY for your offer, AND Is intended to result in revenues in the long run. Here are 3 examples of free things you can sell:

- 1-on-1 Service such as a Free appointment (this could be a consultation appointment for an $10,000 offer.)
- A Group Program like a Webinar which makes an $2,000 offer
- A digital product; something downloadable that will get them to take action in the future (product or service.)

After you have shown the final price and you are now ready to get people to take action, there are 3
components to make an offer. You need at least one of the 3 to make it a successful offer:

1. You have your hard hitter, the "Get it while it lasts" offer, usually done for limited space, X# of products, or special pricing. You MUST be authentic here, or don't do it.

2. This is sharing the possibilities of what will happen when they buy. The Opportunities that you will have will be exponential, inspiring, (insert their values here.) Think of a beer commercial, are they selling beer or are they selling women falling from the sky?

3. The "Financing" or "Money Saving" Option. "If this is something you truly want, we can work out some type of financing options." OR "if you pay in full we will be offering you an X% Discount."

5. Saying "Thank You"

This is my favorite one of all, this is the #1 Money maker...that's right! Saying thank you makes you more money. Let me poise 2 scenarios:

Senario #1: You visit a website and you purchase something, and right away you get an upsell.

Senario #2: You visit our website and you purchase a $500 strategy session with us, and the very next thing we do is say "Thank You" truley from the bottom of our heart. And we ask you if you want to get EVEN MORE out of your session we will offer you 50% off to upgrade your session to a Strategy Day for just $1,500 more.

Now whether you choose to buy the upgrade or not is beside the point here, (we will get to that in the next point.) How much better did the second one feel because we thanked you for choosing to work with us?

The scripts are too long to put here in the book, we (currently) have 5 scripts to say thank you.
You can download them (No pesky opt in required) at:
http://invertstrategies.com/tyscripts/
The Basics are: Thank them, Congratulate them, Ask them to share and give them a next step.

6. Offering an Upgrade

This is going to follow all of the rules of the "Call To Action" plus a few others.

Congrats on buying X. You're going to get (Benefit, Benefit, Benefit.) You will be getting that (Time till arrival)
I know that you're committed to your success with (Solution to problem that offer solved), so I wanted to let you
know about (Upgrade).

Offer: [Solution Framework - how will this solve their problem] You will get all of the benefits of the (original offer) plus it will solve (symptom, symptom, symptom to problem) and you will (benefit).

Scarcity: Do's & Don't - (Why do they want it, {and why don't they want it} [disqualifier to get higher quality opt in's])
Call to action: (A clear and concise single call to action.) What are they going to do next?

7. Follow Up to ADD Value

Do you like repeat customers? Ok that is a really dumb question. This is how you get them to come back and order again and again and again. PLUS it's also how you get referrals from those customers.

This follows the principles of the "Thank You" plus a gift to bring them back into the funnel.

You're Awesome because:

Thank you for:

My gift to you is: (No opt in required)

Click to access:

Once they get it, then they will have an option to upgrade.

First we never "Handle" objections we always resolve them. Second an objection is simply a concern for the return of benefits the person will receive from your offer, so they don't have the belief in its ability to perform.

The 5 major Concerns people will express to avoid telling you their real objection :

(Someone may try to run the same pattern more than once, or cycle through multiple of these objections)

1. Not Enough Time
2. Not Enough Money
3. It's not the "RIGHT" time
4. "Maybe if I could just try it (all for free)"
5. [Buyers Remorse] I just didn't like what I bought, it wasn't what I was looking for. {I was looking for a miracle cure}

Is (Objection) the only thing that concerns you? (repeat until you find all concerns.)
So if I understand correctly your have concerns with (repeat ALL objections they mentioned.)
So let me ask you (get **YES** or **NO** from these, if they go into a story it's a NO)

Do you understand (it) [~10%]

What part or parts don't you understand? (re-explain part(s) they don't understand)

Do you believe that it will/does work (for anyone)? [20%]

Why is it that you don't believe it will/does work? (Show case studies, or offer a Guarantee)

Do you believe that it will/does work for you? [50%]

Why is it that you don't believe it will/does work for you /(Your Business)? (offer a guarantee, and include something that will comfort the client in the success of what you're offering them.)

Now that you have given the solution to their real objection, it's time to address their concerns. Revisit their "symptom" objections and find out if they're still there. If they are then it is that they don't believe it will work for them because of that objection.

Here is how to resolve them:

Time: We can take on X amount of the work, we will need you for Y time, and your team for Z time.

Money: Let's break it into phases and that will make the payments more manageable for you.

Right Time: Doing it now will cost you X, doing it in (A Time) will cost you X + Y + (Z Time). We can get it started and do it in phases now and you can save a lot of time and money, which would you prefer.

Try it: When have you had success just trying something, we can (guarantee) so it makes it a no brainer.

***[Buyers Remorse]: ALWAYS resolve this concern BEFORE you get paid, this will save you in the long run. Simply share the expected results, this is usually "Imagine X, Y, & Z when you have A"

Are you wondering about the last 20%? They will simply never buy from YOU (Your Company) and won't say why.

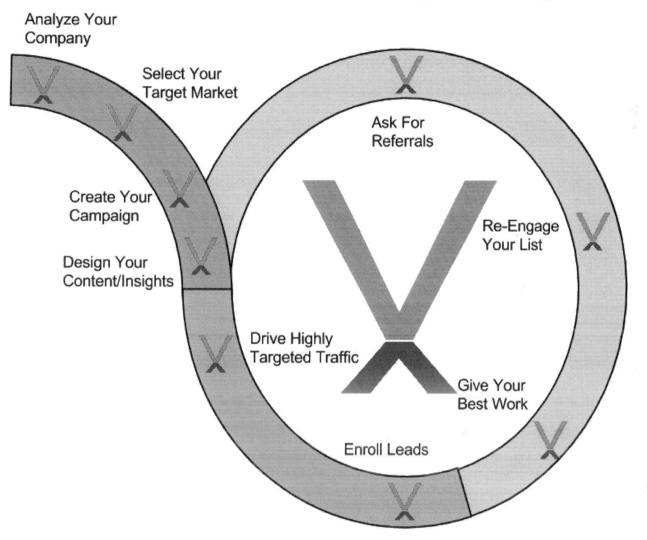

Analyze Your Company

Select Your Target Market

Ask For Referrals

Create Your Campaign

Re-Engage Your List

Design Your Content/Insights

Drive Highly Targeted Traffic

Give Your Best Work

Enroll Leads

Attract:

Analyze Your Company Culture & Customer Experience
- Your company culture and your customer experience go hand in hand.
- Your customers are attracted to why you're in business, and what values are in alignment with their beliefs.
- Understanding your values and the values of your customers is a vital part of your company.
- The culture inside your company must reflect the experience that you promise your customers.

Select Your Target Market
- Understanding how to solve the most urgent problem of your customers is how you get your foot in their door.
- You can have multiple target markets, just not on a marketing campaign.
- Each campaign has its own target market to focus on.

Create a unique campaign for each target market
- Creating a target market is very simple, think of the problem, and 3 ideal people who have the problem you solve.
- Use those 3 avatars to pinpoint similarities and differences between them, you now have a target market.
- You can only choose 2: Quality, Speed, or Affordability for the product/service you will provide.

Record Your Videos, Design Your Pages, & Create Your Campaign
- Start with the goal in mind when creating your campaign, videos, and pages.
- It's easy to record a video, but it takes work to record a great video. Make sure that you use the right equipment for recording.
- Each video you create is paired to a page that gets it a specific result, and drive people to complete the next step in your process.
- Everything you do, from the type of video to the color of the text, has an impact on who will buy, how much they will spend and how long it will take them to make a decision.

Convert:

Drive Targeted Traffic To Your Website & Store

- Affiliates and joint venture partnerships are a great way to drive traffic.
- Ads on Facebook, YouTube, Linkedin, Twitter, and targeted magazines/articles both online and offline.
- Email, call, text, and send snail mail to your current list and past clients.
- Ask your past clients to share with their friends and colleagues.
- Use remarketing to bring people back to your site who didn't take action.
- Anyone can drive traffic to your website, you can send over 1,000 people to any website for under $20, but it won't generate revenue. That's why we send targeted traffic to your site.
- A great question to ask yourself "You have $20. Would you rather have 1000 uninterested people visit your site, or 1 highly targeted person who wants to buy what you offer?"
- Consumers love coupons, promotions, sweepstakes, contests, and free gifts.

Enroll Prospects To Buy From Your Company

- Having a sales strategy is important to every campaign, as a matter of fact it's the most important part of your campaign and often overlooked.
- For clients you have appointments set with send them an email reminder 7 days, 2 days and the day of.
- Give them a call and/or text to remind them of their commitments. (Have a 3rd party service do this to lower your costs.)
- You need to know exactly what you're going to do once you get their email, phone, address, birthday, and other special info.
- The largest sales are made when you know how you're going to help them get what what they want and need.
- People only give objections to buying when they don't understand what you offer, they don't believe what you offer works, and/or that it will work for them.

Magnetize:

Give you best! Give your ALL!
- Deliver on your promise to your customer.
- Offer a guarantee, even if it seems like a small guarantee to you, it provides your customers a sense of security.
- Deliver on time or early every time.
- Deliver on budget or below every time.
- Deliver a higher quality product/service than you promise.

Re-engage them every 5 to 10 days to upgrade or buy more.
- Connect with your customers and prospective customers on Facebook, Linkedin, Twitter, or wherever they hangout.
- Give them a call, a text, a message on social media, a mention in a post, or send them an email every 5 to 10 days.
- People are more likely to buy after they see you connect with them 3-5 times and as many as 12 times total.
- Always thank them, give them something, and then ask them to buy again.
- Ask them to give you feedback with a survey or poll; give them an incentive to give you their valuable time.
- Create campaigns around holiday promotions, special events that your customers are excited about.

Ask them for referrals and reward them for it.
- When they trust you, they like you, and buy from you, ask them to share you with their friends.
- Have a referral rewards program where you give your current customers something special for referring you to new clients.
- You can give them cash, store credit, a free gift, bring them out to lunch, send them a thank you card, or just ask them.
- Look at what other companies do to get referrals and pick one. We chose to give between 10% and 50% of the first sale, based on the item, to the person who referred us to our new client. It's really a low cost of marketing to us.

Want to do this Online?
Complete this online and get the report in your email
http://InVertStrategies.com/Analysis

InVert
Strategies For Your Success

Confidential Application

First Name *

Last Name *

Cell Phone # *

Email *

Business Information:

Business Name

Street Address 1 *

Street Address 2

City *

State *

Postal Code *

Business Phone

Years in Business

List Your Website(s)

InVert
Strategies For Your Success

Please briefly describe your business:

what are the products/services you provide?

Select which strategies you use for marketing

Video Marketing
Webinars/Teleseminars
E-Mail Marketing
Direct Marketing
Joint Ventures/Affiliate Marketing
Networking
Live Events
Print Media Ads
Radio/TV Ads
PR & News Releases

Newsletters
Trade Shows/Vendors/Sponsorships
Social Media
Telemarketing

What are your biggest challenges when it comes to marketing and sales?

○ Attracting quality leads and getting more client with effective marketing
○ Implementing profit generating strategies
○ Finding the right support
○ Finding joint venture partnerships and collaborative entrepreneurs

What systems or processes do you lack in your business?

How much time do you have dedicated to your business currently?

InVert

Strategies For Your Success

What is your big "Why?"

What is an important goal you want to complete in 90 days?

What is an important goal you want to complete in 12 Months?

What is an important goal you want to complete in 3-5 Years?

How much income do you need to feel financially free?

How much revenue do you need in order to have a good lifestyle

Where do you see yourself financially 12 months from now

What are your current sources of income?

About How much revenue did your company bring in last year.

Please select one ▼

How much revenue do you project this year.

Please select one ▼

Describe 3 to 4 Specific Major Sale and Marketing Goals you are working towards and you would like to accomplish with the help of The Magnetic Marketing Company?

What is that missing link that will bring you to success?

Why would you be a good client?

☐ "If I'm accepted to work and it's a good fit I'm willing to do whatever it takes to have a successfully marketed company."

Marketing Analysis

How do you follow up with potential customers who give you their contact information?

Email
Direct Mail
Blog/Social Media
Phone Call
Text Messaging
Networking
I need help with follow up
N/A I just don't

How do you keep track of customers?

CRM (Contact Management) System
Email Marketing System
QuickBooks or Other Accounting Software
Manually
Spreadsheet or Document
I Don't use anything

About how many contacts are in your marketing database?

Please select one ▼

Please choose the option that best describes how you use email to follow up with your list.

I follow up to my entire list by email
I follow up with automated emails
I have advanced email follow-up
I use advanced email marketing
I don't communicate with email.

What do you do to "Magnetize" (or WOW) your new customers?

I deliver a quality product
I give them quality service
I fulfill on-time or early if possible
I follow up with an email
I send a thank you note
I send a small gift
I call the customer to check-in and thank them
Nothing at all right now.

How do you encourage repeat sales?

I use email to communicate to customers
I use direct mail to communicate to customers
I call my customers
I use social media to notify my fans and followers
I have a customer loyalty program
I sell additional product/service at the point of sale
I'm not really sure how to get repeat customers

How does your company handle customer referrals?

Referrals are a significant part of the way our company grows
We have an existing process to ask every customer for referrals
We consistently thank customers who refer others
We have a formal incentive program to reward people who refer
We don't have a system in place.

How do you ask happy customers for referrals?

Social media
Email
In person
Phone call
Customer survey
Referral rewards program
We don't ask for referrals

Target Market Analysis

Demographic Info	Avatar #1	Avatar #2	Avatar #3	Target Range
Example: Age	24	39	44	24 to 44 Years Old
Name				
Age				
Gender				
Race/Ethnicity				
Location				
Income				
Education				
Homeowner/Renter				
Household Size				
Marital Status				
Hobbies				
Mindset				
Company				
Title/Position				

Baseline Price Point Methodology

The Baseline price point is the price a customer will purchase at from you and most other companies over and over.

The event industry is one of the most predictable and easiest converting systems ONCE you use this methodology.

You're sponsoring an event, and that event costs $1,000 for regular admission and $1,000 for a VIP upgrade. The hotel is about $1,000. The round trip flight is about $1,000. What is the customer baseline price point? $1,000.

The question is how you get them to purchase what you have to offer for $2,500. There are 2 ways to do this. The first is to offer a lower price of $1,000 with an upsell for the $2,500 offer. The second way to do it is to offer 3 payments of $1,000 with a $500 pay in full discount.

There is also the ninja trick to offer the $1,000 initial offer and upgrade to the second offer for just 3 more payments of $1,000. Your next offer is for a $10,000 offer and you offer payment plan of $2,500/mo for 4 months plus a $1,000 deposit.

3 Parts to Every Profitable Funnel

1. Products	**2.** (1-on-1) Services	**3.** (Group) Programs
a. Packages	a. VIP Days	a. Events
b. Memberships	b. Exclusive Services	b. Webinars
c. Affiliate Offers	c. Personal Support	c. Telesummits
d. Goods	d. "Help" by Email/Chat	d. Classes
e. Tangible Services	e. Coaching	e. CEO Roundtable

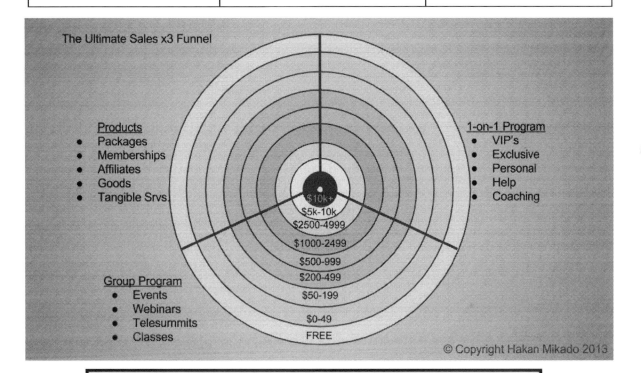

The Ultimate Sales x3 Funnel

Products
- Packages
- Memberships
- Affiliates
- Goods
- Tangible Srvs.

1-on-1 Program
- VIP's
- Exclusive
- Personal
- Help
- Coaching

Group Program
- Events
- Webinars
- Telesummits
- Classes

$10k+
$5k-10k
$2500-4999
$1000-2499
$500-999
$200-499
$50-199
$0-49
FREE

© Copyright Hakan Mikado 2013

Want these in color and Full Size?
Download the full workbook at:
http://InVertStategies.com/HandBook

The Pricing Grid

There are 3 different price guides that are followed based on the type of offer. As you will see they always follow the same structure in all 3 types of offers the price range is the only thing that changes. Use the pricing grid below to determine where each of your offers falls in the price point to see if you're missing a huge gap in sales.

What we have found is that there is about a 10% gain in trust between each offer sold. So for instance if you have a 50% conversion rate on offer #1 you will have about 55% conversion rate on offer #2. (Note: This is 55% of the original 50% that purchased offer #1, not 55% of the total leads. This equates to a 27.5% total conversion rate from all leads.)

Based on average conversion rates starting at 20%, we found that using the pricing structure in conjunction to having all 3 types of offers for the B2P will result in about $100,000 in revenues over 5 years for every 100 leads who claim offer #1. (B2C is $10,000 & B2B is $1,000,000 in revenues over 5 years per 100 leads)

Offer:	Business to Consumer	Business to Professional	Business to Business
Offer #1	Free	No Cost	Complimentary
Offer #2	$0-5	$0-50	$0-500
Offer #3	5-20	50-200	500-2,000
Offer #4	20-50	200-500	2,000-5,000
Offer #5	50-100	500-1,000	5,000-10,000
Offer #6	100-250	1,000-2,500	10,000-25,000
Offer #7	250-500	2,500-5,000	25,000-50,000
Offer #8	500-1,000	5,000-10,000	50,000-100,000
Offer #9	1,000-2,500	10,000-25,000	100,000-250,000
Offer #10	2,500+	25,000+	250,000+

The Ultimate Sales Funnel Worksheet:

The Ultimate Sales Funnel^3

A: _____

B: _____

C: _____

~~~~~~

#1: <u>FREE</u> : _____

#2: $____ - ____ : _____

#3: $____ - ____ : _____

#4: $____ - ____ : _____

#5: $____ - ____ : _____

A   B

#9
#8
#7
#6
#5
#4
#3
#2
#1

C

Want these in color and Full Size?
Download the full workbook at:
http://InVertStategies.com/HandBook

This is great to have your team do so that you can get an understanding for what they're good at; what new products, services, and programs you can have them offer to your customers.

1. Discover Your Gift/Expertise
What is it that you're an expert at?
What are your strengths?
What does the public see you as a leader in?
What can you do with your eye's closed?

2. Explain Your Gift
(Use the worksheet on the next page to do this as a practice.)
Be concise and keep it simple.
A descriptive and catchy title (& subtitle) is what catches the eye.
Include No More than 3 main points and 3 sub points for each.
Make sure that you always have a call to action

3. Make An Offer
Making your offer is simple, send emails, post on social media, ask your past customers, ask your current customers, this is key because this is where you find out if people actually want it, or if they want changes before they buy.

4. Get Customers
Once you have made your offer and got any kinks out this part comes naturally. Be ready to accept credit cards. You will want to tell them the Estimated delivery date so they're expecting it later.

5. Design Your Product or Services
Now that you have all these new customers for an offer you don't have created yet, it's time to design it.

6. Deliver To Your Customer
Once the product is ready to go, deliver the offer!

7. Repeat With A New Product or Service (or with the same offer later)
Self explanatory, just keep doing this. Think of Apple, & Samsung. They come out with a new phone every 6 to 12 months, they follow this brilliantly.

A few months back Apple broke it's record in sales with the iPhone 6 having 4 million PRE sales within 24 hours of announcing the pre-sale opening.

Title: _____ Price: $_____

Subtitle: _____

Main Point #1:_____
    SubPoint:_____
    SubPoint:_____
    SubPoint:_____

Main Point #2:_____
    SubPoint:_____
    SubPoint:_____
    SubPoint:_____

Main Point #3:_____
    SubPoint:_____
    SubPoint:_____
    SubPoint:_____

Call To Action:_____

The Essentials of Deliverability Both Online & Offline (including your employee's understanding):

It may be odd to you that "Your employee understanding your strategy" are all under marketing, deliverability, email, etc. In this section we intentionally combined the system and the people to show how they relate to each other. It will give you an understanding of why your people are more important than the strategy.

Email Basics:

Keep your concepts and wording simple and short. Be straightforward and to the point.

There are 3 major components to consider when you send an email, in the following order:

1. The number one most important part of your email is the length. You want to keep it to less than 300 characters, and if possible less than 150. Ideally it will be less than 13 sentences including the "why I'm Reading", "The problem & solution", the offer, results/benefits and proof, plus your Call To Action.

2. Your reader is going to look at it on a smartphone or tablet so you need to know what it looks like for them. Your sentences should be short, and any images need to be responsive (adjust size based on the screen). If you fail to do this you're going to lose up to 70% of your customers. (our current average for emails read on smartphones.)

3. The email is ALL about them so you better be talking WITH them and only them. Mass emails feel very cold and impersonal. With the technology we have today there's no reason to have emails that look like they're sent to 100,000 people, unless it's a promotion, sale, or newsletter AND still then you can put their name in it.

   How often should you be sending emails to someone? This is really dependent on your business and sales cycle. As a general rule we follow is no more than one every 3 days. You should also consider other ways of getting in contact with someone. By phone, via social media, in person, etc.

Your List Building & Cleansing:

The strength of your list is proportionate to the customers in your funnel. If you buy a list of 10,000 people who don't know you, they don't care about you. But if you nurture your community both online and offline with resources and gifts, they will respect you and love you for it, and getting 10,000 people won't take long. People on your list will move companies, change their email, get a new phone, move, get married, have kids, have more kids, and my point is that you can't know what's happening with everyone on your list UNLESS you ask them. Send them a quick, easy to click questionaire.

Literally 1 question with an A or B choice, and do that every few months. When they click you track what they like and send them relevant emails, that way they don't mark spam or filter out your company. The second part of your list deliverability to it check on a regular basis for bounced emails, especially with B2B when people move companies their email may no longer be valid, check Linkedin for their new email. If they're bounced emails, even if they are getting to their inbox you want to remove them from your list. Send them a private message and let them know you got a bounce error on an email you sent them, and can they please add your contact to the "safe sender" list, this may help, other emails just won't ever get to them if it's their business email. For instance most banks massively filter emails so they have a huge un-deliverability rate.

Another key component to making sure that you're list is interested in what you offer is taking into account the last action they took to send them their next step. If they haven't bought from you in 6 months you don't want to send them the same thing as the customer who just bought a week ago, and vise versa. Make sure the customer experience is customized.

The last and I think the most important part of your email marketing is make them personalized with your mass marketing. "What? Personalized and Mass Marketed?" Yes, use as many Merge Fields as possible. For instance if you meet someone at a networking group, your emails shouldn't just be, "Hi NAME, it was great to meet you." Instead it should be "Hi Name it was great to learn about you and your position with COMPANY at THE EVENT NAME. I would love to catch up with you and learn more about SOMETHING THEY SAID.

Sure this takes about 60 seconds longer to put them into your CRM, which will save you face in the future. You will never forget how you met them, what you talked about, and what company they were working for. Everything you need is now at your fingertips, and they got the "personal" touch. Guess what? Your next automated email might mention one of those things like the event name or something they said.

Opt In's:

When it comes to opt in's there are so many rules to follow and ways to keep your list pure and segmented properly. The key to an opt in is a balance between quality and quantity. We've found that in all cases where someone refused to give their first name with their email it results in a no-sale. So in the least ask for both their first name and email.

The first offer is your "I'm willing to gift it to you and trust you're giving me valid info, if you want to get the bonus materials you'll have to confirm your email address." We don't make anyone confirm their email in order to get to the "Value Add" thank you page which teases them about the gift in their email. But if they want to get the gift they opted in for they do have to confirm their email. Once they've confirmed their email we send them offers for other gifts, and again DON'T require an opt in at that point.

For instance if you opted in to get a digital copy of this handbook you will also be offered 6 other complimentary products, services, and group programs so that we can get a better understanding for what you want. AND you won't have to opt in for each one. We may have you give additional info like a phone number or address. Depending on the market you're in depends on the amount of contact info you want to ask from someone. The list below will build on itself so all of the parts from the B2C will be in B2P and the parts in the B2C & B2P will be in B2B.

(options in parentheses are optional but recommended for higher quality)

- Business to Consumer
    - First Name
    - (Last Name)
    - Email
- Business to Professional
    - Phone
    - (Address)
- Business to Business
    - Company
    - Title/Position
    - (Income)

You can also ask other info (like age, race, sex, etc.) or specialty questions based on your offer.

Frequency:

The frequency in which you contact someone and when you email them about an offer are vastly different. You want to think outside of the box and market to prospects and leads in more than one way. Ideally have 2 online and 2 offline.

See the table below on how often you might want to contact a lead. (This is the MAX):

Sales Cycle:	Business to Consumer	Business to Professional	Business to Business
90 days or less	1 per day	1 every 3 days	1 every 5 business days
3 to 6 months	1 per 7 days	1 every 10 days	1 every 2 week
More than 6 months	1 every 10 days	1 every 2 week	1 every month

Here are 11 Alternative marketing avenues other than email:
You need permission to send some of these.

1. Text Message (Social Fuse)
2. Voice Message - Automated call
3. Phone call
4. Pay Per Click Marketing
5. (Facebook/Twitter/Linkedin) Social Media Direct Message
6. Facebook call them
7. Tag them in a photo or post on social media.
8. Post card
9. Attend an event they attend
10. First class/overnight envelope.
11. Record a video and send it to them

Creative attention grabbing ninja tricks & techniques:

In order to do this you will need the prospects full contact info and be connected on Facebook, Linkedin, and Twitter.

Jack is one of your highest valued prospects you have. You want to make him feel special. So you record a quick 2 or 3 minute video and you speak directly to Jack. You say something along the lines of: "Hey Jack, It was great to meet you at that event last month. ....You had mentioned some initiatives you wanted to discuss with me can we set up a time to speak. ......etc."

You then send them a message with the link to the video on each platform (wait a couple of days between posting on each platform), If they don't respond you set up an ad with only him/her on the list, and you have that video follow him/her around everywhere until he/she completes the action you want or opts out. (The best conversion is for a 1-on-1 meeting)

1. The Essential Messages

The three essential messages are the foundation of Linkedin marketing. These messages must do 3 things.

1. Share why you're contacting them and how you got in contact with them.
2. Add value and ask them about their specific position in their company.
3. Add more valuable and ask for an audience off of Linkedin. Either by phone, in person or on a webinar.

2. Target & Connect

Targeting your prospective leads on Linkedin is very easy. Click the "advanced" search feature and target the demographics you want to connect with.

3. The 3 Touchpoints to Engage Your Connections

The three touchpoints use the essential messages you have created.

1. Connect
2. Ask questions to get to know them
3. Add value to them

4. Give A Gift

Once you've added value with a resource you use, you can gift them something from your company. This is usually one of your opt in gifts, but you're not going to ask them to opt in because you already have their contact info.

5. Intrigue, Inspire & Convert

Once you have their attention do your standard sales process to make your sale.

6. Magnetize Them (Deliver, Make New Offers & Ask for Referrals)

Now that their your customer make sure to simply wow them!

7. More on Linkedin Marketing

Watch this demo and download a more in depth Linkedin overview at InVertStrategies.com/liondemo

There are many different campaigns your company can use to attract, convert and deliver to your customers. Outlined here are 7 of the most effective solutions and what they're good for. Each one of these campaigns has been designed with consumer behavior in mind, but will be customized to your company's unique needs and concerns. Any single component of the campaigns below can be moved, removed, or combined to give your customers the unique experience your company provides:

Note: Projected ROI is based on investment for the system which you drive properly targeted marketing, at a cost of $3.75 per opt in, and selling only a $47 offer to about 20% of those who opted in to receive your gift. The benchmark ROI for Marketing is around 1.8x (180%) These numbers are statistically average, we have strategies that have helped clients get a 20x (2,000%) ROI.

1. **Lead Capture Campaign**
   - Industry/Stage: All businesses with an online presence that want to market via email and keep people updated.
   - Campaign Spend: $3,500-$5,600
   - 6 to 12 Month Projected ROI: 400 to 1000 Leads, $6,000 to $15,000
   - Process:
     - Create an opt in video and page. Keep it simple and to the point.
     - Send them to a thank you page and ask them to share with their friends.
     - Give them a gift on a page with another offer.

2. **Consultation Enrollment Campaign**
   - Industry/Stage: Leaders/Coaches with a $2,000+ package offered during a 1-on-1 session.
   - Campaign Spend: $7,600-$11,500
   - 6 to 12 Month Projected ROI: 2,500 to 10,000 Leads, $13,000 to $20,000
   - Process:
     - Start with a lead generation video and page details benefits of having a consultation.
     - Thank them for opting in and give them greater insights into what they will get during their consultation with your team. This further qualifies them.
     - Have them complete an application that helps you understand what their needs and wants are, and assess their interest level.
     - Have them schedule their appointment online using a scheduling software.
     - Thank them for scheduling a time to speak with your team, ask them to share on facebook, and give them a free gift.
     - Send them to a page with your free gift, and offer an upgrade or cross sell.

3. Insights & Content Delivery Campaign

- Industry/Stage: Real Estate & Financial teams with 5+ deals a month
- Campaign Spend: $14,500-$22,500
- 6 to 12 Month Projected ROI: 4,000 to 15,000 Leads, $26,000 to $40,000
- Process:
  - Share your what you will teach them about in the next video.
  - Thank them for opting in and teach them about the most common problem that you solve for people.
  - Teach them what to do to avoid the problem, and offer to work with them.
  - Outline the benefits of working with your team, and your company.
  - Have them complete an application to qualify them.
  - Have them schedule a conversation with a member of your team.
  - Thank them, ask them to share with their friends.
  - Give them a pdf or webinar to get more info.

4. Storyboard Campaign

- Industry/Stage: Service based businesses that want to share their story, why their special, what makes them unique. Help them stand out as the expert in their industry
- Campaign Spend: $18,000-$27,000
- 6 to 12 Month Projected ROI: 5,500 to 20,000 Leads, $32,000 to $49,000
- Process:
  - Share your story to people who care and want to know more about your company, express why you're in business, why your unique, and what are some of the success stories you have, then ask people to join you.
  - Thank them for opting in and give them some insights about what you can help them with, make an offer to solve their problems.
  - Outline the benefits of working with your company, and have them complete their order.
  - Thank them for ordering, ask them to share, and give them a free next step resource.
  - Send them to your next step resource and ask them to upgrade on what they just bought.

5. Commercial Campaign

- Industry & Stage: retail companies with 1 location with $1+ million yearly that are looking to get customers into their store.
- Campaign Spend: $19,500-$29,000
- 6 to 12 Month Projected ROI: 7,500 to 25,000 Leads, $37,000 to $57,000
- Process:
  - Your commercial outlines why you're the right company to do business with and positions you as the expert in the industry.
  - A whiteboard video outlines your professionalism, and character of your company right on your main website.
  - They are then sent to your vision and success stories video where they learn more about your company, why they should buy from you, and satisfied customers.
  - An opt in video that shares valuable insights on the products you sell, and offers a gift in store.
  - Thank them, ask them to share, and send them to claim their gift.
  - Give them insights on best practices and demonstrate around your products.
  - Make an offer for them to receive a gift card in exchange for their address - Send them a postcard with a voucher to claim their gift card at the customer service counter or at checkout.
  - Thank them for taking advantage of the offer and let them know they can get a second one when they buy $25+ in gift cards right now.
  - Send them to checkout, thank them for their purchase if they do.

6. Product/Offer Launch

- Industry & Stage: Workshop Leaders & Speakers who are hosting a major event in the next 6 months who want to turn their event into a complete home study course and market it for residual income and asset protection. OR Companies with a new product/offer coming out in 3 to 6 months.
- Campaign Spend: $39,000-$77,000
- 6 to 12 Month Projected ROI: 15,000 to 40,000 Leads, $72,000 to $139,000
- Process:
    - A commercial designed to create intrigue around your new product.
    - The whiteboard video is created to post on a blog sharing the functionality and benefits of your new product.
    - The opt in video is crafted to share about the pre-release of the product, and for them to get special updates only available to subscribers.
    - Thank them for registering and give them a sneak peek at the video series.
    - The next day send them an informative video outlining the major benefits, uses, and keys to success.
    - Offer a special early bird pre-order price.
    - Followed up by (4) videos that expand on a single component of your offer.
    - Each video refers to the final video where the offer will be made.
    - The final video brings the components off all the previous videos and expresses how they all work together. Make an offer on a pre-order price, higher than the early bird pricing.
    - Thank those that purchase, ask them to share, give them a free gift or webinar training.
    - Explain the webinar/gift and are presented with an upgrade option.
    - They claim the webinar .

7. Ultimate Campaign

- Industry & Stage: Companies with multiple teams/locations with $10+ Million yearly revenues, who want to increase their revenues by 10-15% yearly.
- Campaign Spend: $67,000-$97,000+
- 6 to 12 Month Projected ROI: 25,000 to 100,000+ Leads, $120,000 to $180,000+
- Process:
  - Connect with people who need what you have to offer in a short commercial designed to build intrigue.
  - Your whiteboard video is viewed on your main website to capture attention and share your ideology.
  - A vision and success video differentiates you as an industry leader, you stand out, beat out the competition, and show people your successes and satisfied customers.
  - Your Opt in video will get people excited to stay informed about your company, and offer them a gift to get them back in the store.
  - Thank them, ask them to share, and send them to claim their gift.
  - Give them insights on best practices and give a demonstration around your products.
  - Make an offer for them to receive a gift card in exchange for their address - Send them a postcard with a voucher to claim their gift card at the customer service counter or at checkout.
  - Thank them for taking advantage of the offer and let them know they can get a second one when they buy $25+ in gift cards right now.
  - Send them to checkout, thank them for their purchase when they do.
  - The following day email them about a special customer appreciation event and special educational video series, send them the registration page.
  - Thank them for registering and give them a sneak peek at the video series.
  - The next day send them an informative video about the event and offer them a ticket in for free when they purchase a gift card or a no-show deposit.
  - Followed up by (4) videos that expand on a single component of your offer. Each video refers to the final video where the offer will be made.
  - The final video brings the components off all the previous videos and expresses how they all work together. Make an offer on a pre-order price.
  - Thank those that purchase, ask them to share, give them a gift.
  - The gift is presented with an upgrade option.

Each video and page has a very specific purpose designed to have consumers complete a single task and get them into a "YES, YES, YES" pattern and then buy. Each type of video and page can be move, omitted, or combined to fit your specific goal for that campaign. Each campaign is structured around the end goal and the actions required of its target market to achieve that goal.

Commercial
Your Commercial is designed to get people from your Video Ad to your capture page. This ad is featured on YouTube, Facebook, Linkedin, and other places you can put your Video

30 to 60 Seconds: Grab peoples attention, peak their interest, make them want more!

Whiteboard
Your Whiteboard video is designed to give a short story about what it is that you offer, provide value and engage your clients with a cartoon video.

45 to 60 Seconds: Put it on your main website. Show your company character.

Opening
Your opening video is for branding and consistent recognition of your videos they get peoples attention and are only about 4-7 seconds.

4 to 7 Seconds: Brand your videos, grab peoples attention, keep this consistent.

Closing/Ending
Your video ending is to add to your call to action and get people to stay informed. Usually done to attract subscribers to your Youtube channel.

7 to 10 Seconds: Ask people to share, and stay informed by subscribing.

Story
Your visual story connects your viewer to you, tell your story, why are you in business, what is your vision, and who has been successful using what you do.

2 to 3 Minutes: Give people a feel for your company, and your successes.

Opt In/Lead Gen

You want people to opt in so you can send them marketing emails and claim a free gift.

45 to 90 Seconds: Tease about the value they will get when they opt in.

Facebook Opt in

Your Facebook optin brings people to a place they know and trust. So when you ask them to opt in from Facebook they will trust you more.

45 to 60 Seconds: Engage people where they trust others most, on Facebook.

Insights/Content

Each Insight/Content video has 3 major parts. Educate them on a problem, share some basics to solve the problem, and offer to solve it for them.

10 to 15 Minutes: Your target market will be happy to buy & DIYers will Share it.

Offer/Sales

Your offer video shares benefits of signing up or purchasing what you're offering.

3 to 5 Minutes: Drive home the benefits and eliminate objections.

Thank You

Your thank you video shows how much you care, it builds trust and gets people to share your company with their friends.

30 to 45 Seconds: It's Simple...Thank them, ask them to share, & give them a gift.

Bonus & Upgrade

Having your bonus & upgrade video is important to give your clients an opportunity to go to the next level with you and it also builds trust at the same time.

2 to 3 Minutes: Deliver your gift and ask them to upgrade or buy something new.

Launch Opt in

You Product Launch opt in video is designed to share what someone will get when the product/service is launched.

45 to 90 Seconds: Hook them back in with interesting info about a new product.

Launch Set

Launch Value Video is to educate and add value to your clients. Seed in the eventual opportunity.

10 to 20 Minutes Each: Solve a specific problem part of a bigger problem.

Launch Offer

Launch offer is designed to offer what you have been sharing about in the previous videos.

15 to 25 Minutes: Connect the problems and offer to solve whole problem.

Launch Enrollment

Launch Enrollment video is to express the benefits of purchasing your product or service from the launch.

3 to 5 Minutes: What are the benefits of enrolling and buying from you.

Launch Thank You

Launch thank you is to express how much you care and are excited to be working with them.

30 to 45 Seconds: Thank them for watching, buying and ask them to share.

Webinar/Livecast

Your webinar/livecast is a great way to attract current and prospective clients to learn and get value from what you teach. You can turn this into an automated and repeatable system that puts sales on autopilot.

25 to 90 Minutes: All-in-One Video to teach, and offer to solve the next problem.

The Ultimate Video Marketing Sales Funnel For List Building & Sales Launch Automation

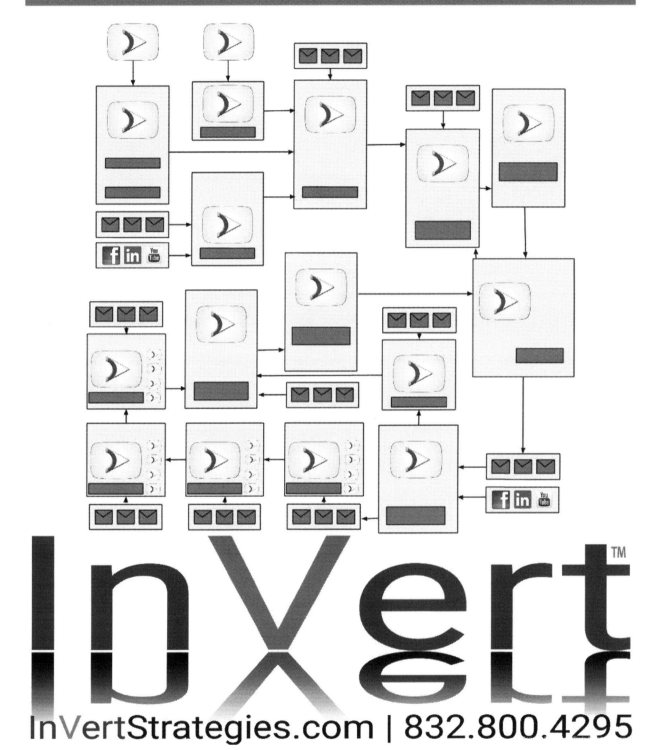

Our Strategic Maps

The Ultimate Video Marketing Sales Funnel For List Building Automation

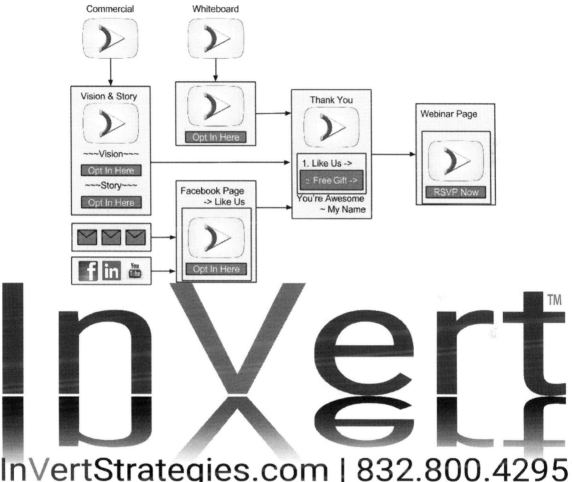

InVertStrategies.com | 832.800.4295

InVertStrategies.com | 832.800.4295

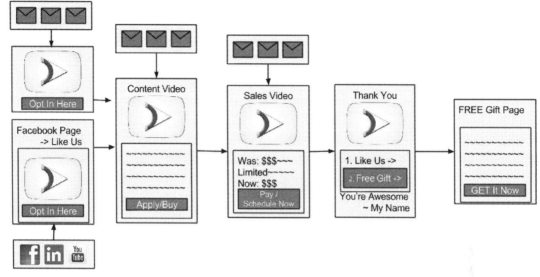

InVert™

InVertStrategies.com | 832.800.4295

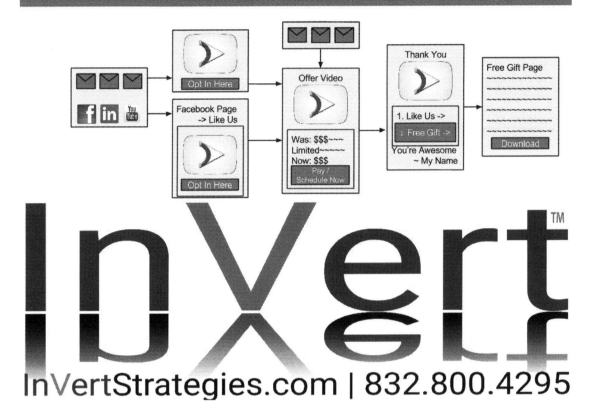

InVertStrategies.com | 832.800.4295

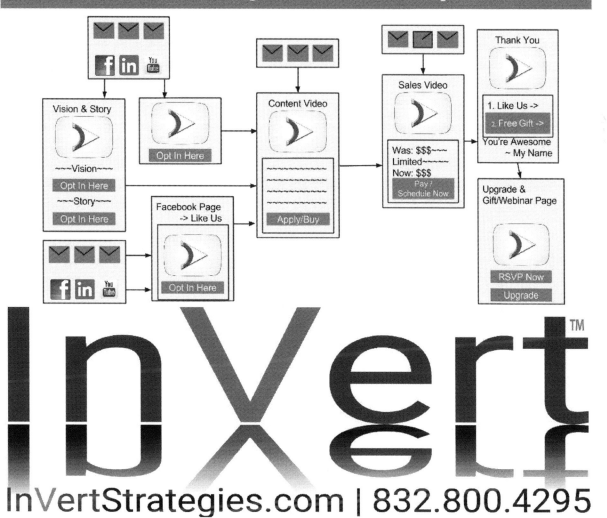

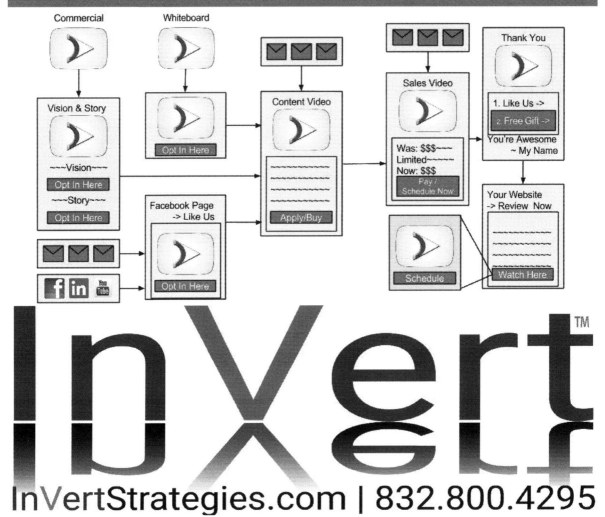

InVertStrategies.com | 832.800.4295

The Ultimate Video Marketing Sales Funnel For List Building & Sales Launch Automation

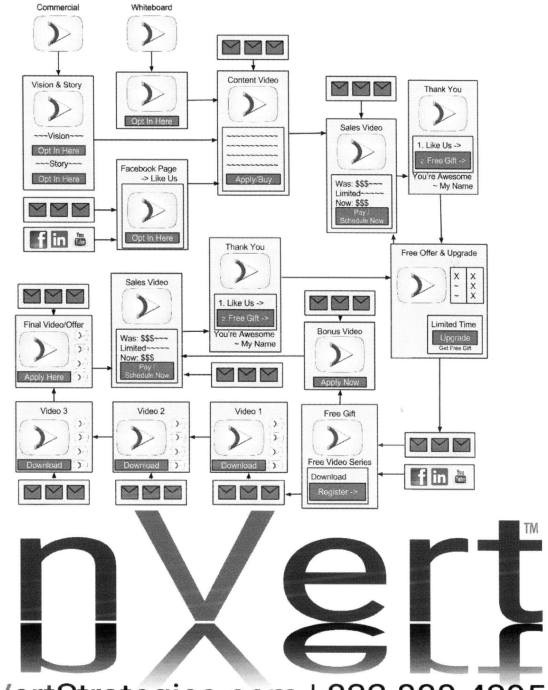

Your Next Step:

Congratulations, you finished the Chief Marketing Officer Handbook. You have more tools and resources than ever before. Would you like another free resource? 85% of businesses don't know how to use their strategy. 60% don't even have a strategy at all. Here at InVert our goal is to get the 60% a strategy and help the other 85% implement so that their business is making profits.

You know someone that has a business without a strategy. They are breaking even and keeping the business afloat and you know that your business can thrive, you're just not sure how.

InVert is here to help: CLICK HERE

Sign up for a complimentary strategy session so that you can work with InVert to build a unique plan for your business and industry. Find what is working well, what is not and how to fix it. We increase engagement with participants by up to 300% & see up to 200% increase in conversions within 90 days. We guarantee our results.

Fill out your business analysis and schedule a time to meet with an InVert strategist to start seeing these kinds of results in your business. InVertStrategies.com/Evaluate

With the Business and Marketing Evaluation we provide the solution to the urgent challenges and problems in your business. We InVert your strategy so that instead of being in the red or just breaking even, we get you in the green.

Only take advantage of this if you want to see up to 200% increase in conversions, increase engagement with participants by up to 300%, and invest in a plan that you will see an ROI on. Don't take advantage of this if you don't want to take 15 minutes to fill out a business application, equip your sales team with the tools to increase effectiveness and efficiency, or spend money on a strategy that will increase your profits and revenues.

Why wait another second to watch a sinking ship? We have the lifeboat and InVert is here to help.

Go to InVertStrategies.com/Evaluate to get started now!

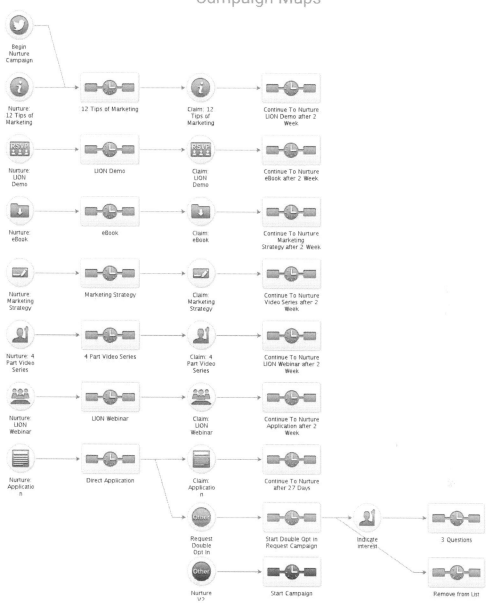

The Ultimate Sales Funnel - $100,000+ ROI Every 5 Years per 100 Leads

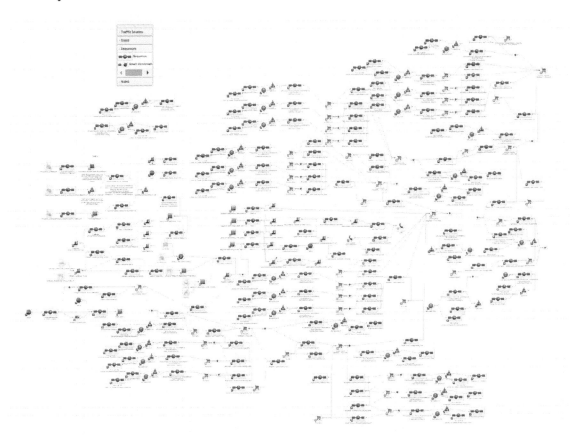

Purchasing Baseline Upsell Segment of the Ultimate Sales Funnel

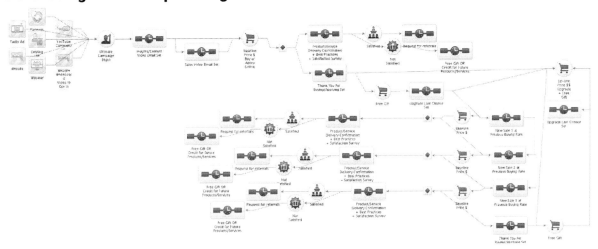

Company Analysis and Customer Entry Campaign
- Part of Ultimate Sales Funnel

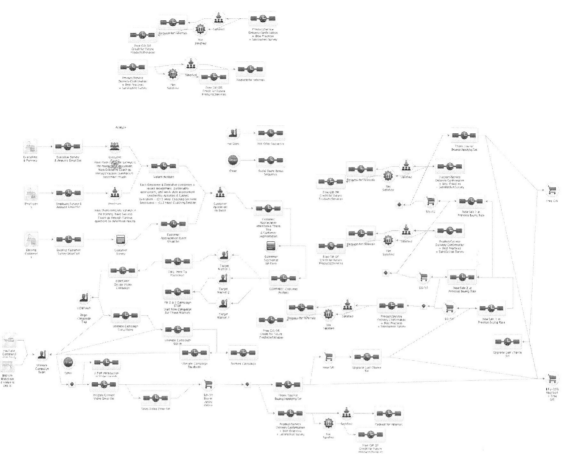

Campaign
Pre-Sell & Lead Entry Campaign

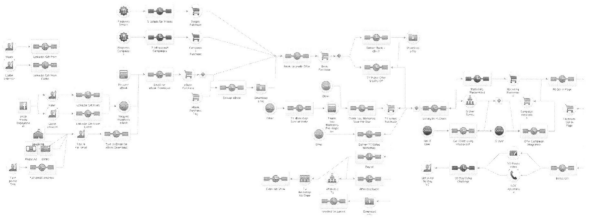

Video Series to Appointment Campaign
- Part of Ultimate Sales Funnel

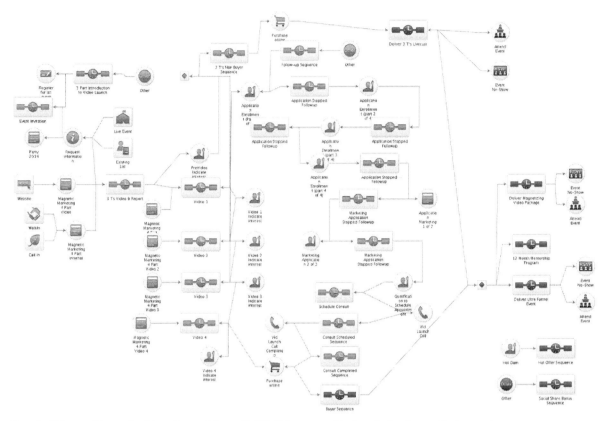

SocialFuse Text In For Speaking & Webinar to Schedule Appointment

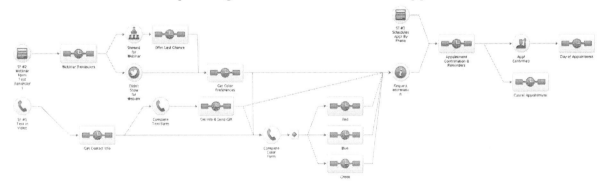

Hawk Mikado, Chief Executive Officer

Hawk is the brains behind the system and the strategy. He designed The Ultimate Sales Funnel and integrated it with some of the most powerful online automation systems in the world. He can turn just about any business he works with into a profit generating machine.

Caitlin Mueller, Chief Creative Officer

Caitlin is the genius behind our copywriting, cameras, crafting the production of video and is head of our creative department.

Production Team

The production team is complied of experts in all facets of video, photography, and visual effects editing. They understand how consumers react to a video, and how to create emotion with every shot. Our team will help you before, during, and after production to get you the results you want to get from the campaign we co-create.

Marketing Team

The marketing team specializes in getting you and your company the best results in traffic generation. They use a combination of ads on Facebook, Twitter, LinkedIn, YouTube, Google, etc. and Targeted Magazines/Articles both Online and Offline.

LinkedIn LION Marketing

Our LinkedIn Marketing Department are masters of LinkedIn Marketing. Our team can grow your list by 300 leads for every sales rep in your company. We grow your list, nurture them on your behalf, and help you turn them into prospects and clients.

Have Questions?
Our Dedicated Team Is Standing By to Help

Whatever you need, we can help. Reach out to us and let's talk.

✉ **Concierge@InVertStrategies.com**

📱 **855.350.4295**

InVertStrategies.com | 832.800.4295

Schedule Your Marketing Evaluation Now! Call 832.800.4295 »

1. Facebook Calling

When connecting with a prospective client on Linkedin or Twitter, you can ask them to connect with you on Facebook. Now this may not always work but when it does you get right to the decision maker without needed to go through the gatekeeper.

You will need 3 things in order to make this work:
1. Facebook messenger on your smartphone
2. Your connection needs to have Facebook Messenger on their phone
3. The knowledge that you can call your "friends" on Facebook via Messenger.

You can go through and start calling your prospective clients directly from facebook and set up a call.

Note: Most people are confused when they see an incoming call from Facebook for the first time.

2. Schedule for My Business Card

Do you give out your business cards like water? And is the purpose of giving someone your business card to set up a call with them or to give them your card so that they can put it in a shoebox? In order for someone to get your business card you can require that they schedule a call with you before doing so. Let me do some math for you so that you can see how much each of your business cards are worth.

As you saw earlier the lifetime value of a customer might average $10,000. The average conversion rate is 20% (that's 1 out of 5). Lets say because you work with us to put systems in place every customer you get gives you 5 referrals. You go out to a networking group and give 5 business cards which results in 5 appointments and 5 referrals. You now have 2 new customers for a value of $20,000 over their life. You gave 5 business cards to get those 2 new clients. $20,0000 / 5 business cards = $4,000 value per business card.

3. Mention Yourself and Your Prospects (in Social Media)

Use the @ on Facebook to tag yourself and/or colleagues on just about every social media. This will also post it on their timeline as well as notify them. here is an example of a post:

@InVert CEO @Hawk Mikado just finished the 2015 CMO Handbook!

Top 5 Paid Business Resources To Automate Your Business & Increase Your Profits:

Infusionsoft CRM System - Automate Your Emails, Sales, and Customer Relationships.
> Visit http://GetMMC.com/InfusionSoft to receive up to $1000 off your KickStart

LeadPages - Simple Website and Lead Generation Page Designer:
> Visit http://GetMMC.com/LeadPages and get a 30 Day money back guarantee.

SocialFuse #1 TXT Marketing Tool:
> SocialFuse integrates into InfusionSoft to do SMS Marketing. Learn more at

http://GetMMC.com/SmsPlayBook

PipeDrive
> Visit http://GetMMC.com/PipeDrive for a simple and efficient Sales Pipeline. Free

the first 30 days and $9/user/mo

Zapier
> Visit http://GetMMC.com/Zapier Unlimited Use for 14 Days FREE. Paid Plans start

at $20.

Top 5 100% FREE Business Resources To Increase Your Profits:

LION Marketing Training - Use Linkedin to Generate 1000's of Leads Each Month

Visit http://GetMMC.com/LION to watch a 90 minute training on how to use Linkedin to generate 100's or 1000's of new qualified and targeted leads each month for FREE.

Google Alerts:

Set up http://www.google.com/alerts to stay updated on what others are saying about your industry so you can keep up to date on your social media posts and blogs.

GRC's HR Automation System:

Visit http://getresultscoach.com/automated-hiring-success to get a FREE 90 Minute training on automated hiring and get $1000 off the full system which includes access to post 100 Jobs on Linkedin as part of the system a total value of $29,900.

JoinMe:

http://GetMMC.com/JoinMe is a great way to share a presentation online with a small group of people, its FREE.

Asana:

This is the ultimate team project and task management and delegation system. http://asana.com

DirectPay Payment Processing & Shopping Cart Options:
For a 4 Week Free trial to a shopping cart go to: http://GetMMC.com/DirectCart
Great rates on your merchant services account to process payments, its the best price we've found: http://GetMMC.com/DirectPay

Google Voice:
Google Voice is the #1 Tool for a sales team, executive office, or even a small business. Up to 5 people per phone line. You can schedule times that the phone rings each person, so you can have your bases covered all the time. You can get texts on it and you can make calls from it on your computer (with the admin account.) Its free for US and low cost for international calls. This is a <u>must have</u> component of your business. http://Voice.Google.com

LastPass:
Keep your accounts secure with this great tool that allows you to share your passwords with people without sharing the information. It also saves and stores your passwords as well so you don't have to send yourself an email or change your password if you forget your login. This one is a big time saver. Always remember that cyber security is important and frequently change your passwords on a regular basis.http://GetMMC.com/LastPass

SignNow:
A simple to use document signing program for both online and tablet use. If you do less than 5 contracts per month it's free otherwise its $25/month
http://GetMMC.com/SignNow

Linkedin:
The #1 Professional Social Networking Site. 80% of users are between the age of 18 to 45 and are earning over $100k annually in their household. About 60% are decision makers. Get on Linkedin. http://GetMMC.com/Linkedin

AirBnB:

Great for your stay when you travel for business, its less and you get to stay with a family. It's usually less of a luxury experience, though you can certainly find some that provide the executive treatment. http://GetMMC.com/AirBnB

Regus | HQ Global Offices:

If you like the idea of a full service office anywhere in the world, Regus in your office. With 3000 (and growing) locations around the world, you can't go wrong. You can actually say that you have offices worldwide. http://GetMMC.com/Regus

ScheduleOnce Scheduling Automation System:

http://GetMMC.com/Meetme is the best automated apointment scheduling system on the market and starts at only $5/mo. Get 14 days free when you visit them online. (they do have a free version with ads)

LeadPlayer:

Do you like to have your video automatically play and pop up a call to action as soon as they're done? We have have seen a 200% increase in conversions because of this tool alone. Get it for $197. http://GetMMC.com/LeadPlayer

Uber:

Need to get someone quick, and in style? Get an Uber, a fun ride share experience. Great to network and you can also ride share with your colleagues. Get a Free Ride (Up to $30) at http://GetMMC.com/Uber

Lanyard:

Find Sponsorship, call for papers, presenters & Speakers opportunities at Events for Corporations, Associations, and Professional Industries.
http://lanyrd.com/calls/

SpeakerMatch:

Do you like to speak, and want to have events find you on a regular basis? Go to http://GetMMC.com/SpeakerMatch it starts at $10/mo

Meetup:

Find events that are local and have your target market. Join the group, attend a few, and speak to the host about speaking at a future event. The regular meeting events are the best. http://Meetup.com

BlogTalk Radio:

Reach out to radio hosts on BlogTalkRadio.com

Eventbrite:

visit http://GetMMC.com/EventBrite to create both online, local and even international events for FREE.

My Top Trusted Advisors

(Mention "Hawk Mikado" and you will get a free consultation with each of their teams)

Angelique Rewers - The Corporate Agent:

The Corporate Agent - She teaches small businesses how to get in front of mid market and Fortune 1000 companies. Contact her at Concierge@TheCorporateAgent.com

Jeff Klubeck - Get A Klu:

Jeff is a lot of fun and he is a great speaker, great leader, and an incredible individual, he teaches communication, leadership, accountability, and sales. You can Contact him at Jeff@GetAKlu.net

Jon Block & Roni Diaz - Here & Now Network:

Jon is incredible and his wife Roni are a great team. Jon works on the business side of things, he is the best niche expert I know, and he can fill a room like no one else. Roni is on the personal side she works with Dharma and gives you a total fashion makeover. You will look hot and feel hotter when you're done with her. Jon@HereAndNowNetwork.com

Todd Roth - Cruise One:

Todd and his team of travel agents are partnered with Cruise One to give you the best rates on your travel. The best part is that you don't have to pay him for his services to book your trip. He gets paid by the company and you don't pay any more. Set up a call with him at http://GetMMC.com/CruiseOne

Daniel Rodriguez - Dr. Budget:

Dr. Budget will get you set up to have your finances on track and in order. I highly recommend if you want to make your finances set to succeed email daniel@drbudgets.com

Gail Kraft - Kraft Bravery:

Kraft Bravery will help you gain a hold of your vision and achieve your goals and dreams. You will have a step by step plan to achieve what you want and a know how of what to do. To learn more email Gail@GailKraft.com

Carl Logrecco - Innovative Inspirations:

Innovative Inspirations is a key to growing your business. Carl is an expert when it comes to joint ventures, building sales teams, designing your $10k+ packages, and having the confidence to ask for it on every call. He will build you a top performing commission based sales team. Hes services are only available after an evaluation with our company. Complete your evaluation at http://InVertStrategies.com/Eval

Works Cited

http://www.sourceforconsulting.com/files/file/Firing%20the%20engines%20of%20growth%282%29.pdf

http://blog.brightcove.com/en/2014/03/now-available-analyzing-roi-video-marketing

http://www.apple.com/pr/library/2014/09/15Apple-Announces-Record-Pre-orders-for-iPhone-6-iPhone-6-Plus-Top-Four-Million-in-First-24-Hours.html

https://www.youtube.com/yt/press/en-GB/statistics.html

http://oncamerasizzle.com/

http://www.adweek.com/socialtimes/survey-49-of-linkedin-users-have-household-income-over-100k/88454

Made in the USA
Lexington, KY
10 May 2015